music

in the

early years

susan young • joanna glover

FALMER PRESS
Taylor & Francis Group

UK   The Falmer Press, 1 Gunpowder Square, London, EC4A 3DE
USA   The Falmer Press, Taylor & Francis Inc., 1900 Frost Road, Suite 101, Bristol, PA 19007

First published in 1998

A catalogue record for this book is available from the British Library

Library of Congress Cataloging-in-Publication Data are available on request

ISBN 0 7507 06597 8 paper

Design by Carla Turchini

Printed by Graphicraft Typesetters Ltd., Hong Kong

acknowledgments:

The following copyright holders have granted permission to reproduce music and words:

Boosey and Hawkes Ltd. for 'Cherry Pie' from *Be a Real Musician* by Geoffrey Russell-Smith. Copyright 1977 to Boosey and Hawkes Music Publishers Ltd. Reproduced by permission of Boosey & Hawkes Music Publishers Ltd.: London.

Essex Music Group for 'Dumplin's' from *Calypso Folk Sing* edited by Massie Henderson and Sammy Heyward in 1963 published by Ludlow Music Inc.. Used by permission of The Essex Music Group: London.

Ward Lock Educational for 'Cuckoo Cherry Tree' from *The Funny Family* by Alison McMorland and Hop Tune-ay (in an altered version), originally from *Brown Bread and Butter* by Alison McMorland. Used by permission of Ward Lock Educational.

Wayland Publishers Ltd. for 'Let us make a ring' from *Dancing Songs and Rhymes* by Iris Grender published by Three, Four, Five Publishing Ltd. 1974. Used by permission of Wayland Publishers Ltd.: Hove, Sussex.

World Music Press for 'Sansa Kroma' as sung by Abraham Kobena Adzenyah and published in *Let Your Voice Be Heard! Songs from Ghana and Zimbabwe* by Abraham Kobena Adzenyah, Dumisani Maraire and Judith Cook Tucker, Tenth Anniversary Edition C. 1997 World Music Press. Used by permission.

Every effort has been made to trace the ownership of all copyrighted material and to secure the necessary permissions, but if any have been overlooked the publishers will be pleased to make the necessary arrangements.

contents

to
Laura and Ellen
Jimm and Annie

acknowledgments

with thanks to
Lesley Flash
Brian Loane
Mary Nicholson
Stephen Ward
Graham Welch

the staff of the
Early Childhood Centre
Froebel Institute College

and all the teachers and children.

photographs: Colin Evans
music copyist: Ivan Craig Victor
photography at these schools:
Broadmead Infant School, Croydon (Headteacher: Christine Johnson)
Broadmead Junior School, Croydon (Headteacher: Michael Brockett)
The Hayes Primary School, Croydon (Headteacher: David Wilcox)
Wattenden Primary School, Croydon (Headteacher: Hilary Leppington)

introduction

This book is intended for teachers working across the three to eight age phase who want to make music integral to the life of the nursery and early years classroom.

Music has often been taught as if it were different, something outside the mainstream curriculum, with teaching approaches quite at odds with early years work. This book takes children's development in music as its basis and works towards building a music pedagogy within early years practice.

Children have a musical vitality, their own way of being musical in the world. The teacher, with an awareness of what is possible, must find a way of meeting children on their own musical terms, yet extending their learning along pathways which are mapped within the wider musical culture.

This book looks at children's music learning. It draws on well-tried practice of many teachers and our own observations and work with children over the long term. A readiness to observe and reflect is central to the listening-led practice which threads through the book. Sample activities model ways of working with children. These have been written in such a way that they can be substituted with other material and adapted by teachers to use with their own resources. Three to eight is a wide age span. Earlier and later stages of learning and progression are described as a basis for matching activities with children's learning needs.

For the child working in music, the divisions between performing, composing and listening are not distinct. In this book sections on movement, singing and instrumental work are based on the child's central ways of engaging with music. Throughout, we have tried to take the teacher's perspective on understanding how to work with the child in music.

Books are full of words. They can convey ideas, pictures, meanings. Writing this book has been difficult without the one thing we are really talking about – the sound – being there.

music in the early years

planning for
early years music

The staff of a West London nursery gather together for their weekly planning meeting. Below is a transcript of parts of their discussion:

'the singing area – we could put out the puppets for some voice games and singing play, and rig up the microphone and cassette recorder – who'll work there with the children? Perhaps we can record some of their voice work? Playing with the puppet might encourage S. to use her voice? she still hasn't spoken since she started...'

'what songs for this week during carpet time? Is it time to teach a new one? And we'll do some voice games this week...'

'shall we put out the glockenspiel on the table with beaters? And hang the new chimes and rattles from the climbing frame outside if it's fine – who will work at the music table with the children using the glock?...'

'nursery rucksack to go home with J. and M. on Tuesday and Thursday – be sure the dual-language rhyme book is in for J. and the new tape of the music we are listening to...'

Notice the many layers of planning which the staff cover in their discussion; typical for any early years educational setting. Organising equipment and people is as important in fostering music activity and learning as are the decisions for teacher led input, what song and what voice games. Notice too how provision is adjusted to meet children's individual needs, for one who has not yet found any voice for the nursery and another who can voice in two languages.

They are planning to cover each of the following areas:
● creating an environment for music;
● observing, listening and responding to children's music and musical behaviours;
● preparing teacher-guided input;
● catering for the learning needs of individual children.

Teachers working with young children in music need a special kind of flexibility. Selected materials and activity ideas are helpful, particularly for planning specific input, but are not enough. An understanding of the principles which lie behind planning for early years music will enable the teacher to make informed decisions.

At the start of their schooling, all children bring with them a rich and individual accumulation of skills, knowledges and understanding of music. If teachers are to build a curriculum directly on what children can already do, they must find ways of discovering their abilities, collecting and using them as a basis for planning.

Coming to know 'where the child is' musically is a process of gradually building a picture over time and from many sources. Information will be gathered in from:
- discussions with parents;
- observation and listening to children in the nursery or classroom;
- planned music activities which are designed to enable the teacher to find out about children's abilities and experiences.

knowing what to look for

Knowing what to look for, what kinds of knowledge, abilities and feelings towards music children might have acquired in the years prior to school will guide teachers in their information gathering. In other fields, such as language and number, early childhood teachers are increasingly coming to understand the sophisticated abilities children have acquired from family life and how these can provide a basis for first teachings.

A similar story of competences for music is beginning to emerge from studies of young children, together with an awareness that teaching approaches must be adjusted to take account of what children bring. Discovering that babies can hear and listen to music in the womb, and when born will recognise the music of their mother's culture in preference to other musics, (Woodward, 1994 and 1996) tells us that children have innate abilities to absorb musical information from all they hear around them. In their earliest years prior to schooling children will have heard a wealth of music in all kinds of places and from many sources: radio, TV, videos, supermarkets, places of worship. Children come to early years schooling steeped in the music of their own culture.

Young children are equipped with acutely sensitive aural skills which can detect the smallest changes of pitch, timing, placing of stress. From earliest days if they are to communicate successfully with caregivers (and on this communication depends survival) they must listen attentively to the voices around them (Papousek, 1996). Equally, they can use their own voices with infinite variation, and are highly successful communicators and voice users even before speech develops.

Children from musically alive homes will have enjoyed traditional children's rhymes, games and songs with family members. Being bounced and jiggled on the knee in lap games lays the foundations of rhythmic awareness. By taking part and attempting to join in with songs and rhymes the children are making their first attempts at using voices in musical ways. And these early experiences of being musically active are wrapped in the warm contact of family. Perhaps not surprisingly, children from these families will grow up singing and responding to music more freely than from children from homes where there is less musical parenting (Kelly and Sutton-Smith, 1987). Modern working patterns may leave little time for childhood traditions of singing and game playing. The television, although a source of music to listen to, is a poor substitute for adults available to respond and play.

Social and cultural differences will result in great variation in the home music backgrounds children have experienced. Each child will have an individual musical identity which they are beginning to piece together from the ways in which music is used in their families and communities and the part they take in music (Siraj-Blatchford, 1994).

The kinds of knowledge, skills and feelings children will have acquired from home life are listed below. Each area is illustrated with examples which try to capture some sense of the variety of background experiences children will bring:

- knowledge of how music is used in their families and communities and their part in that musical activity; *song singing used as an expressive aspect of parenting; spiritual music listened to in silence in the place of worship; joining in, singing along and dancing with the radio in the kitchen.*

- knowledge of songs and rhymes learnt in the home: from family, friends, other adults, the media;
  snippets of Disney film songs learnt from a video;
  traditional lap-clapping game learnt from a grandparent.

- knowledge of how music from their own culture sounds, an intuitive understanding of its musical elements;
  listening to a Welsh male voice choir rehearsing;
  watching Hindi films and hearing the film songs.

- knowledge of home spoken language, dialect and possibly an additional language;
  the sounds and rhythms of their own language.

- knowledge of instruments, the way they are played and the kinds of sounds they will produce;
  pop-group instruments seen and heard on the television;
  hearing an adult practising an instrument at home.

- knowledge of materials and ways of making sounds from a range of materials and objects;
  tapping, banging play objects to discover the resulting sound.

- physical abilities, the feel of how the body moves, its rhythms, strengths and timings;
  action clapping game played with carer;
  dancing to Bhangra music with older sibling.

- aural abilities, the discrimination of fine differences in sound;
  being interested in sound for sound's sake, playing with sound-making objects.

- vocal abilities, using their voices in many ways;
  playing voice games, experimenting with variations of voice sounds.

- feelings towards different forms of musical activity, a sense of themselves as musical people.
  encouragement (or not) in their first efforts at singing;
  family pleasure in singing a happy birthday song;
  attentive support at first efforts to play an instrument.

discussion with parents

There is a growing appreciation of the importance of parents as the child's first and continuing educators and of the valuable insights into their child's prior learning which they can provide for teachers (Steirer et al., 1995). Holding conversations with parents in which they can gather information enables teachers to begin to understand the range of the child's previous experiences of music. On this foundation they can build continuity of experience for the child and ensure that what is provided reflects and values the child's cultural background (Robson, 1996).

observing and listening

Observing and listening to the child in music can help teachers to build a real understanding of 'where they are' which will help them plan music for each child.

Paying concentrated attention to what the child is really doing is one of the most difficult things for a teacher to do. It takes time, organisation, energy and a certain disposition to set aside preconceptions. Paley writes from her experiences as a nursery teacher, 'I was a stranger in the classroom, grown distant from the thinking of children' (Paley, 1990:15). And as adults we may be strangers to the child in music and have grown distant from children's musical thinking. Listening to children in music can challenge many long-held beliefs about the way music should be taught and what the long-term aims of music education are. The following describes one teacher's experiences:

 Mary Nicholson, a nursery teacher in Wandsworth, planned a regular weekly slot to observe one child, over one term, playing one instrument, first claves and then a glockenspiel.

Each ten minute session was tape recorded. Mary listened to the tapes later and made notes. This in-depth focus on one child provided her with insight which she might not have gained from more superficial observations of several children in general activity. She writes, 'I have worked with one child throughout, either on her own or with other children. I have shared far more with her than I ever envisaged and have learnt from her. Having the opportunity to work with one child in this way has given me an insight into the world of music making for the young child. It has helped me to develop a sense of what the child experiences at this stage of development.'

This caused Mary to reflect on her teaching role, 'Initially my role in this (the observation sessions) was to echo the patterns on a similar instrument in order to reinforce the recognition process. This was clearly an adult agenda, arising from the need to teach in some way. I imposed this adult agenda, and to some extent it was successful in that the child was able to create musical patterns and recreate them in further sessions. In hindsight using this sort of approach as a starting point is limiting. When we free ourselves of the reins of adult-led sessions and enable the child to evolve her own agenda the potential for exploration on the part of the child in conjunction with an adult is far greater' (Nicholson, 1995).

Later Paley writes, 'Paradoxically, as the focus shifted from me to the children – what do children think about in the classroom? – I began to see my own role more clearly' (Paley, 1990:15). Looking closely at children's activity can allow us to come to understand more about their music; it can also highlight teaching which is less effective than the teacher had imagined. Mary Nicholson continued to partner this child closely, but modified her teaching approach considerably in line with what she came to understand.

This model of listening-led teaching for music, in which careful observation of what the child is really doing guides teaching, threads its way through this book.

The following section looks in closer detail at starting music with a new class. It suggests an approach to planning in which setting up diagnostic activities for assessment and differentiation is woven into the ongoing work of the classroom.

starting music with a new class

Meeting a new class at the beginning of a school year brings a mixed brew of feelings – of optimism, trepidation, a sense of fresh opportunities and new starts – and the challenge of needing to get to know each other quickly; for teachers and children alike. Both energy and adrenaline levels can be running high.

It is worth recognising this transition period clearly for what it is; from the point of view of music this settling in time can be fruitful in several ways if carefully planned for:

● the teacher can plan activities which allow her to hear and see something of the musical experience and capabilities children

bring with them; future planning can be matched to these;
- music is a good vehicle for getting to know children in a multi-faceted way;
- musical activity is a useful way to bring a new group of children together as a group and to reinforce a sense of community in the classroom.

Music is also a very broadly based subject and is best taught in a climate where it is part of a whole learning environment – along the lines of how language is catered for – rather than confined to a single lesson slot once a week. The first few weeks is therefore a crucial time for introducing the range of musical opportunities and expectations.

The first half-term's work can be planned with all these factors in mind:
- it can be new work, aiming to stretch the children and move them on;
- it can have carefully thought out 'diagnostic' opportunities built in.

The latter need not be specially set up tasks or tests, simply planned-in ways of observing children engaged in a range of ordinary musical activities. And these activities can be designed to help everyone get used to working as a class together and to renew or establish relationships all round.

activities

assessment and differentiation

- make a class song tape containing lots of solo contributions, particularly children's own spontaneous songs and a few short songs sung altogether to 'see how we sound as a class';

  Listen for and work on:
  voice skills;
  musical structures used in song compositions.

- as a class, in a circle, make a 'taking turns and joining in' (see p.171) instrumental piece once a week for 3 weeks, a third of the class at a time; discuss the range of instruments in use; the listening two-thirds of the class discuss with improvisers each time how they heard and thought of the music;

Listen for and work on:
*instrumental skills, interactive skills – musically and
socially, musical imagination;
range of vocabulary and ways of talking about music.*

〜 as a class and in groups, listen to three given pieces of music on
tape and agree on one to listen to again; discuss why it is a good
choice.

Look for and work on:
*attentive and detailed listening;
understanding of music heard – elements;
how the music affects me as a listener;
range of vocabulary and ways of talking about music.*

planning the basics

Music works best when it is a part of daily life in the classroom. For
many activities 'little and often' is the key to success. Children's
natural enthusiasm for music makes it invaluable at coming-together
times and as a way of helping the class to work as a social group. A
song or some listening can be lively or calming alternatives to a
story. Just enjoying the sound of sounds, a musical game or a newly
-made composition can lift the mood of the whole group. Music in
school can contribute to the quality of life just as it does outside it.

The more flexibility that can be managed in planning opportunities
for music, the better. Music learning involves a very wide range of
activities and these need planning for in different ways. For
example:

- singing: *with the whole class, in smaller groups for work on
  skills, in pairs using song cards;*
- playing instruments: *individual work with structured provision,
  in small groups with a teacher or helper, accompanying class
  singing;*
- composing: *composing songs individually or in a class or group
  time; composing alone with an instrument; using the computer;*
- moving: *class work in hall time;*
- circle games: *with a small group or the class seated in a circle;*

- listening to music: *with the class as for story time; individually or in groups on headphones; on a video; or as an audience for a live performer.*

Young children move easily between the activities of composing, performing, moving, listening and appraising. Development of musical skills, knowledge and understanding also crosses these boundaries and planning should take account of this. Musical activities should be integrated where possible e.g. a composing activity followed up by listening to recorded music; listening to and appraising a tape recording of class singing.

Music has often been seen as a class activity e.g. singing together, with little monitoring of individual learning within this class setting and little opportunity for children to work by themselves or benefit from musical interaction with the teacher one-to-one. Planning work in different formats can give children more scope for practising skills and working with their own ideas at their own level. It also allows teachers to build in strategies for observing children and assessing their learning. The range of formats might include:

- teacher-led work with the whole class: *teacher input, class participation and opportunities for individual contributions or taking turns so that children are heard individually;*
- small group tutorials with the teacher or a helper: *planned activities in a music corner or round a table allowing differentiation between children and one-to-one musical interaction and talk;*
- individual play: *structured opportunities for free play; provision for bringing findings to share at a 'carpet time'; some observation or 'partnering' by the teacher;*
- individual or paired work in music area: *for more experienced children, opportunities for composition or practising with instruments; provision for saving work on tape; staffed by a 'listening helper' (e.g. a parent/carer, a pupil from a local secondary school).*

If working in music in these ways is new to the school, the organisation and resources for this kind of provision can be introduced gradually. Developments can be planned for and need not all take place at once.

During the early years, musical progression depends on planning that differentiates enough to take account of the skills, knowledge, understanding and cultural background that each child brings and that matches teaching input to the child's learning needs. Planning curriculum content therefore is a matter of bringing together a knowledge of the areas which need to be covered with ongoing observation and assessment. As in all curriculum areas, teaching needs to be flexible enough to draw activities from the planned scheme and introduce them at appropriate times.

The later sections of this book discuss the kind of opportunities which can be provided in each main area of the music curriculum, outlining, as it were, the 'musical map' against which planning takes place. Each section also looks in some detail at strategies for observing and assessing children in each area with indications of what to look for and how to move children forward. This assumes an approach to teaching music which continually moves between the roles of:

- providing planned opportunities for music learning;
- observing and listening to children's work;
- noticing indicators of what is needed next;
- assessing learning with the children;
- choosing activities from the planned scheme of work which will move children forward.

This approach requires that during the process of planning activities, teachers build in:

- learning objectives that are clear and that can be made explicit to the children;
- strategies which will allow teachers to listen and observe individual children;
- clear ideas of what to look for in assessing progress;
- opportunities for assessment.

Involving children in assessment of their own learning is important if they are to develop their own understanding of what they are aiming for. Even with the youngest children, teachers can identify and discuss in simple terms one or two key objectives, e.g. *we're going to see if we can sing 'Twinkle, twinkle, little star' with us all keeping together* or *we're going to practise the jump for our voices when we sing 'twinkle, twinkle'*. Children can then be involved in assessing how well these objectives were met and what made it easy or difficult. This can be done in a way which both registers achievements and always looks forward as well, e.g. *'we finished together very well at the end; it's hard to keep together all the time because you have to listen to everybody else and remember the song as well'* or *'finding that second note and singing it just exactly right is going to take lots of practice; we'll remember to try a voice-jumping game later on'*.

The teacher's agenda for assessment will be wider than the one shared with the children. Carrying out assessment whilst activities are in progress is not always easy, although it draws on the habit of observation that early years teachers apply in almost everything they do. Observing individual children does not, of course, imply that this is done only in one-to-one teaching situations. In a class situation it requires building in opportunities for hearing what individuals are doing, though some of this may be done while several children are playing or singing at once.

Nor is it possible to track all children all the time. Strategies of taking 'spot checks' round a group or focusing on a few children only within any one activity can be used. This works well enough as long as care is taken that over a stretch of time each child has had some close attention, however brief, across a reasonable range of activity. Observation is always easiest when it is clear what is being looked for, hence the need to clarify this as part of planning. As long as the teacher has a second sense which is open to picking up the unpredictable outcomes as well as those aimed for, this works well. It is also useful to remember that progression in music cannot be thought of in a simple linear way. Music learning is multi-dimensional; understanding develops within an expanding network of criss-crossing skills and knowledge, many of which are interdependent.

In order to secure continuity of learning, music planning will need to take place between groups of teachers and the whole staff of the school. Ideally, the process of developing a music curriculum will always involve:
- some 'hands on' music workshop sessions for teachers as a group working together: *out of these can be developed some agreement about approaches to music in practice;*

- establishing a vocabulary in which to talk about music: *this emerges most easily from workshop sessions as above and is crucial in being consistent with children;*
- trying out new, jointly planned activities: *a group of teachers try these out with their own classes e.g. of different aged children, and come together again to evaluate the work;*
- listening together to samples of children's work on tape: *joint discussion helps to clarify what expectations are, what the range of ability is, issues of differentiation and progression.*

It is not possible to develop an agreed and effective scheme of work until there is a good basis of positive classroom practice in music which is already underway and in which a majority of teachers are involved. If this is supported by the kind of staff development strategies listed above, a climate of ongoing development evolves to a point where a scheme of work can be meaningfully prepared. This will outline long-term plans for each term and year group and bring ideas for resources and materials together with learning objectives and focuses for assessment. Neither the scheme of work nor any published resource scheme the school has can do more than provide half the picture, however. Working through a series of pre-planned activities without re-shaping work on a basis driven by observation of children and differentiation accordingly can severely reduce the quality of music learning. Unfortunately, the block by block sequence laid down by many schemes of work can't encompass the demands of a non-linear subject.

Some system of recording and profiling children's work is needed to support continuity, particularly at points of transfer, and reporting. This needs to be both effective and minimal. Once again, if this consideration is built into the planning of all music work, it can be more easily managed. Provision can be made for:

- a simple check system recording the child 'visiting' the range of specified activities: *this ensures that no one misses out one or more areas of the music curriculum;*
- notes of significant achievement kept on individual children: *these can be very brief but need to cover work across the different areas of music i.e. composing, performing, listening and appraising;*
- child or teacher choosing to save examples of work occasionally: *work can be saved on tape; this is straightforward once the use*

of tape recording becomes a familiar part of music work;
- end of year statements bringing together assessment of learning in each aspect: *see 'assessment points': p. 183.*

endnote

Above all in planning, it must be remembered that music is a creative art. Space must be kept within planned activity for children to work creatively for themselves. Teaching approaches must treat children's creative ideas as intrinsically valuable and as an essential component of development. This is not a sentimental vision drawing on vague ideas of being left to express oneself. Creativity is an energy that both drives and is fuelled by the acquisition of skills and, above all, understanding. The introduction of new skills and knowledge must work with, and not counter to, this energy. If the concern to foster the child's own musical 'voice' is lost, then in a central sense, the work has lost its meaning.

playing games

music in the early years

We can't and needn't define exactly what counts as a game; but we can all recognise the value of gathering up a store of small games – focused activities – which children can enjoy and return to again and again. Such activities have, in varying mixtures, elements of fun, play, joining in, being caught out, thinking quickly and reacting to the unknown, practising and testing skills, co-operating and accepting a role in a group. Musical games help children to interact musically, listen hard, increase perceptual and motor skills, grasp concepts, remember musical patternings, invent ideas, experience music in a group and build self-confidence in all of these. For the youngest children participating and contributing, knowing when to or when not to, are early group music skills which are woven into the fabric of games.

Games offer a framework, often defined by a set of rules, and this sets a challenge whilst maintaining reassuring boundaries. Sometimes the framework acts as a container for creative contributions, sometimes it builds in the unpredictable: interacting with other people, taking a turn when you don't know it's coming or reacting to chance situations. Sometimes it simply challenges skills, memory or understanding.

Playing again and again is part of the essence of games. Children's tolerance and enjoyment of repetition is greater than adults'. Much of the value of the game is absorbed only once the game is learnt and becomes familiar and fluent. New games can be discovered or invented and added to an ongoing repertoire. The collection of known games belongs to the group. Revising familiar games over and over again for as long as they're enjoyed and effective is important if children are to reap the benefits. In some games, the intrinsic value is a musical experience in its own right; in other games, a single musical skill can be isolated for practice within the flow of the game.

The teacher sets the psychological climate of the game. The child who feels safe and relaxed, who is not coerced into joining in, and who is confident of enjoyment and some success when taking part, will become fully involved and ready to take risks. The teacher has the role of managing how the game develops and keeping an eye on all the children taking part. The teacher is both participant and an observer and has to oversee the pace, flow and dynamics of the game either taking a lead or standing back as required.

The following suggestions are for games which could be adapted and extended. They are grouped according to musical learning purpose, (indicated in brackets). Above all, the teacher needs to be clear about 'what's in it', what the value is, what is to be learnt.

listening games

These focus children's attention, improve concentration, encourage sensitivity to particular aspects of sound. They might lead on to listening to music which shares some of the features indicated.

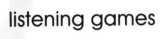

activities

Listen!

⤳ Make silence, listen for the sounds around. Are they far? near? Where do they come from? What kinds of sound?

(AWARENESS, SENSITIVITY, CONCENTRATION.)

Hum!

⤳ Hummmmm – find humming voice, pick up a note and hum it , fade to silence.

⤳ Listen to the sound until it fades.

(QUALITIES OF SILENCE, CALMING, CONTROLLING THE SOUND.)

Where?

⤳ In a circle, all sit with eyes shut. Two children change places. Point to where footsteps are heard.

(SENSITIVITY TO DIRECTION OF SOUND.)

Bear's Honeypot

⤳ Blindfold bear who guards his honeypot. Others try to steal without the bear hearing.

(SENSITIVITY TO SOUND, TO CAUSING IT.)

Can you...?

⤳ Put scissors on a tray without a sound.

⤳ Pass around some bells so that they barely make a sound. Children can invent challenges for each other.

(HANDLING SKILLS AND CONTROLLING SOUND.)

Presto!
- React with a single clap to a sound made, for example, two stones tapped together.
- Do the same with eyes shut. Hold the silence in suspense.

(QUALITIES OF SILENCE – EXPECTANT, LISTENING FOR.)

rhythm and pattern games

These develop listening, recognition, memory, and the skills of co-ordination in performing and inventing rhythms and patterns of all kinds. They might lead on to focusing on these same skills in the context of singing a song, composing or hearing recorded music.

activities

Fill the gap
- Children sit in a circle. Everyone claps three times and leaves a space. Do something in the gap – stand up, touch your toes, wave a hand.

(KEEPING IN TIME WITH OTHERS, SENSE OF THREE CLAPS AND TIMING.)

- When everyone can do this, go round one by one.

(WAITING, KNOWING WHEN, TIMING.)

Copy Me
- In a circle. Make a simple body percussion pattern and pass it one by one around the circle. Keep the rhythm, keep the tempo.

(LISTENING AND WATCHING, REMEMBERING, KEEPING TO A TEMPO.)

Pass it around
- Pass a teddy around the circle. Get used to taking and passing and the rhythm of this.
- Pass a beanbag, dropping it on the floor in front of the next person each time, hearing the small sound it makes.

(LEARNING TO PASS, FEELING THE PATTERN OF PASSING, PASSING RHYTHMICALLY.)

Round and round
- A drum sits in the middle of the circle. Say or sing the rhyme together. Pass the beater in time with the rhyme.

⚡ When the rhyme finishes clap a rhythm for the beater holder who copies the rhythm on the drum.

Pass the beater round and round (x3).
If the beater stops at you, you can make a sound.
[tune of London Bridge is falling down].

(LISTEN, REMEMBER AND REPRODUCE A RHYTHM PATTERN.)

In twos, threes and fours

⚡ Sit on the floor and tap once on the floor and once on knees: 1-2;
Do the same, but now with two taps on knees: 1-2-3;
The same but extend to three taps, four taps;
Call out a number and the pattern must change.

⚡ Same game but facing a partner. Tap knees and clap hands together.

⚡ Make up chains of different number clapping groups. Watch and guess.

(KEEPING A STEADY BEAT, GROUPING BEATS (METRE), RESPONDING AND CHANGING, SENSE OF DIFFERENT METRES.)

Signals

⚡ Make up some rhythm signals e.g. 'stand up', 'sit by me', 'find a space and lie down'. Make sure the rhythm patterns are all different. The game is made more difficult if a couple of patterns are almost the same.
Children listen and follow signals.

(LISTEN, RECOGNISE, DISCRIMINATE.)

pitch games

These practise discriminating between different pitches, hearing the relationships between them, and voice pitching. These can be linked to the kind of activities suggested in the section on 'music with voices', in preparation for song singing and improvisation.

activities

Same or different

⚡ Choose a pitched instrument and agree a single note for the child to play.

Is the note I play the same as your note? Same or different?

(LISTENING AND MATCHING PITCH.)

High-low

~ Use high C and low C, and the words 'I can swing high, I can swing low, high, low, low, high'. Make up a sequence of these elements, patterned in any order. Children follow with arm swings and try not to get caught out.

(FEELING HIGH AND LOW WITH BODY, LABEL LEARNING.)

Stand up, sit down

~ Two notes moving up say 'stand up'. Two notes moving down say 'sit down'. All follow the musical instructions.

~ Make the jump smaller to make the game harder.

(PITCH DIRECTION.)

dynamic and timbre games

The following games help children to recognise small differences of timbre and dynamics. They should then be encouraged to apply this sensitivity in their own music making and listening.

activities

Your sound, my sound

~ One child makes a sound, voice or instrument. The next must match the sound of the child before exactly and make a new one.

(LISTENING AND MATCHING VERY ACCURATELY.)

Egg shakers

~ Three or four egg shakers of different colours (each colour has a very slightly different timbre) in an egg box. Bring out one by one, listen, shake, put back.

(SENSITIVITY TO TIMBRE.)

Find the pairs

~ Pairs of film tubs filled with identical materials. Children listen and match up pairs.

(FINE DISCRIMINATION OF TIMBRE AND MATCHING.)

Say it more softly

~ ...and again more softly, and again more softly, and even more softly then in your head, again in your head

AND OUT LOUD! (just once)

~ The same with a small sung pattern.

(CONTROLLING VOICE DYNAMICS AND HEARING IT IN YOUR HEAD.)

Warmer – colder

~ Hunt the thimble, the music guides you, playing louder or softer.

(LISTENING AND RESPONDING TO GRADATIONS OF DYNAMICS.)

Listen and shake

~ Two rattle sounds which are quite similar (or bell sounds). Shake your hands for one and your feet if you hear the other. Practise. Then do with eyes closed.

Signals and *Round and Round* can be adapted to focus on timbre.

Games can be fitted into small moments of the day or, as suggested above, can prepare the way for music making or listening activities. Introducing a small number of games and staying with these over a period of time helps a new class develop musical cohesion and is the first stage for teachers in adjusting activities to match skills.

This is the first experience for small children of behaving musically in a social setting with others listening. This in itself is an early performing skill.

talking about music

When we move into a new field of activity, we move into a new sphere of language use (Wittgenstein, ed. Barrett, 1978). Whatever musical activity is taking place, talking with children about music plays a key role in teaching and learning. For both children and teachers, moving into work in music brings with it the need for certain sorts of talk and some specific vocabulary. Talking about singing, moving, playing instruments, composing, performing, representing and listening to music all require familiarity with ways of using language in a musical context.

Sometimes we feel a resistance to talking about music at all. There may be a sense that talking somehow diminishes the experience, that the music itself is what matters, or that there is much in music which simply cannot be said. Such feelings relate to our sensitivity to music and to a valuing of the musical experience, in the moment, as being importantly beyond words. We should hold on to this. Indeed, it is something which can itself be discussed with children. Sometimes when the music stops, we don't want to speak. And we certainly don't want to start taking the music apart in a cold and analytical way for fear of spoiling it. So when to talk and when to remain silent is an issue in itself for teachers.

If teaching is to move children forward, however, and to increase their understanding, skills and knowledge, talking is clearly an indispensable part of that process, as it is in any subject area. If songs are just sung and there is never any discussion of the songs themselves, how they might be sung, how they've been composed, the context they come from and the voice skills needed to sing them well, the learning process will be slower than a school curriculum can allow time for. For some children, the learning process will never get underway at all. Alongside the use of movement and of other ways of representing music, talking is a central foundation for the process of music learning.

It is through using language that children's musical understanding is able to move from an intuitive sense of how music works to an articulate basis for the ongoing development of musical comprehension. As children gradually become able to conceptualise and describe musical processes and structures, and to grasp the ways in which we think of and respond to musical experiences, so they are able to develop their own musical purposes and voice.

Teachers need to be confident in using a basic music vocabulary and clear about the different ways in which music can be discussed. Children can then be introduced to both, quite explicitly helping them to build their own awareness of language use in a musical context. Learning to communicate about music, as well as through it, is a vital part of musical development. Children cannot become independent in this unless they are given models and the skills through which to communicate for themselves. Learning to talk about music must be seen as a key part of the teaching agenda with early years children.

In this section, an outline of different kinds of talk about music is given. The talk may be taking place in any kind of music learning situation e.g.

- talk about a song that has just been learnt;
- talk about a very simple piece played by the teacher or composed by a child;
- talk about recorded music listened or danced to.

the role of the teacher

Children must feel at ease if they are to participate fully in talking about music. The teacher needs to create a climate in which contributions are listened to and valued and in which children can feel supported rather than exposed. Whether as a composer, performer or listener, music is very closely tied to our inner sense of ourselves. In these contexts, self esteem can be very much at risk. Discussions about music often require that objective and subjective aspects are brought together and there must be a sensitivity to this from both the teacher and the whole group. Children cannot use talking times to explore and express their feelings in relation to music unless they feel safe to do so. This is a matter not only of careful handling of what children say, but also of giving time and encouragement for thoughts, sensation and emotion to be put into words.

Creating a positive climate for musical talk rests to a considerable extent on the teacher modelling the roles of speaker and listener in this particular context. Teachers can show through their own behaviour how thoughts and feelings can be shared and how the individual can respond appropriately to what others offer. As in all teaching, body language and facial expression are crucial and quickly convey to children how music is felt and understood and how at ease the teacher herself is in such a situation. The teacher needs to take an active role in using language and be confident to take a lead, talk to the children and tell them things when appropriate. This is particularly important in the early stages while children find their feet. Asking what may well be a very unfamiliar kind of question (e.g. 'what did you hear?' or 'how did that make you feel?') and waiting for the children to come up with some sort of answers can in itself lead to a rather uncomfortable atmosphere.

The teacher will need to:
- listen carefully;
- give children enough time to formulate their ideas in words;
- ask questions which grow from how the children are thinking;
- model ways of talking about music and our responses to it;
- give vocabulary, information, explanations and interpretations;
- adapt inputs to meet needs as they arise;
- be aware of body language.

These are all familiar teaching skills, used across the whole curriculum. Applying them in a musical context enables children to learn how to talk about music and to take part confidently in group discussion.

building a vocabulary

If the school as a whole can agree a list of simple vocabulary in which to talk about music with children, this helps to ensure consistency and continuity as children gradually build their language skills. Most terms used will be familiar to teachers, although precise meanings and applications may need some clarification. This is best done by the staff as a whole talking about music sung, played or listened to together.

Children can be encouraged to talk about music using whatever language they have. Building on this, as in any field, specific vocabulary is introduced alongside those experiences which give it a context for use. Having the vocabulary enables a child to begin to conceptualise the musical idea; having the musical experience is essential if the child is to make sense of the words. There is no virtue in delaying the introduction of musical language.

A simple music vocabulary can be based on consideration of each of the main elements of music in turn. These elements each have their own embedded sets of metaphors and images. Encourage children to draw on the richest possible variety of words and to use these in conjunction with the more centrally musical 'terms'.

introducing music vocabulary based on musical elements

Timbre: *the sound of sound, the quality of the sound itself.*
Use any adjectives which can conjure up sound. Of all the elements, timbre is arguably the hardest to find words for. The timbre of a sound might be described as scratchy, smooth, ringing, hollow, piercing, rich, clanging, whispering, sparkling, breathy, harsh, resonant....and so on. Onomatopoeia is invaluable here; children can invent their own sound words. In fact, any kind of poetic description can help to get inside the sensation of different sound qualities. Timbre is so closely tied to the quality of how we physically perceive sound, with our whole bodies as sensors, that descriptions often draw on these physical responses too.

Duration: *the length of sounds, both their natural decay time and their length as patterned in the rhythmic aspects of music; the length of silences and rests.*
Use words which help children to grasp the time-based aspect of sounds and of rhythms. These often borrow the mathematical vocabulary of time, number and measure. Movement words such as 'jumpy', 'swinging', 'marching' help to characterise rhythms based on particular groupings of note-lengths.

Single sounds can be compared and described as 'longer than' or 'shorter than' other sounds. Sounds may die away gradually or stop short; they may be 'damped' i.e. stopped before their natural end.

Musical rhythm may be based on a steady beat, with an underlying feeling of a regular pulse which may or may not be heard. Much rhythm vocabulary relates to the length of notes in music measured against a beat. It might be useful to describe:

- the pulse, feeling the pulse;
- steady beats, no beat;
- rests or silent beats;
- beats divided in two or three.

Notice that rhythm may also be free, with no regular beat at all. In this case, talk about how the music moves: freely, faster, slower and how silence is used.

Dynamics: *the drama of the sound; in particular the relative loudness or quietness of the music and the way this alters as the music develops; silence and accents.*
Use the words louder and quieter (avoiding softer which is possibly confusing) comparatively where possible, or qualify to try to be clear about the degree to which music is loud or quiet. It is common to talk about dynamic 'levels' and in some music dynamic changes are sudden, as if it had jumped from one level to another. Silence often has a particular quality; it can be startling or restful according to context and it is useful to try to describe this too.

Pitch: *the highness or lowness of the music; the dimension in which melodies are shaped.*
Use words which draw on the metaphors of space and movement in space. Children find this one of the hardest areas to conceptualise and using the analogy of physical movement up and down in space seems to help, particularly if supported by visual representation as well. Standard musical notation uses the same convention, showing melodies as moving higher or lower on the stave. Again, high and low are best treated as comparative terms. Describing melodies calls for describing them as lines and shapes, and as moving by step or by jump, twisting and turning. The overall contour of a line might be described as jagged or smooth. The way we think of melody relates it to a mapping process in every sense. Part music and harmonic ideas are thought of in terms of vertical space, one part above another; chords are built of notes stacked up, happening simultaneously.

Tempo: *the speed at which the music moves.*
Children easily confuse tempo or speed, which is measured against a beat, with aspects of duration. There can be a steady tempo, i.e. a steady underlying beat, whilst rhythm patterns use increasingly shorter, and therefore faster sounding, notes. Use movement words to describe tempo as, for example, fast, lively, a walking pace, lazy, slow.

Texture: *the quality produced by the number of layers in the music and how close together or far apart they are.*
Musical texture might be described as thick or thin, sparse or intricate. A texture might be a single line, single notes one at a time; or it might be layered, with different parts moving together or at different times. Lines might be closely woven together or spread out. Pitch, timbre and rhythm as well as structure all contribute to musical texture.

Structure: *the overall shape of the music as a whole or within sections of it; how the music is built.*
Use words which describe how the music is put together: phrases, sections, repetitions or that refer to parts of it e.g. beginning, middle, end. Verse and chorus, call and response, are standard song structures. Structure can be thought of architecturally as how music is constructed, or as the drama of how music changes over time.

describing music in musical terms

This is the aspect of talking about music which many people find most daunting. As a listener, it is often more familiar to talk about whether we liked the music or how it affected us. Describing music in its own terms is crucially important in giving children a core understanding of how music works and in helping them to make choices as composers or performers. Describing must be unhitched from making judgements. Describing the music might be viewed as:

- saying what was heard;
- saying what happens in the music as it goes along;
- saying how the music is constructed.

In this kind of description the focus will be on the elements of music: timbre, duration, pitch, dynamics, tempo, texture and structure. The aim is to build children's understanding of how each element is used in constructing the music.

Again and again, when working with music we come up against the problem of its invisibility and the fact that it is a time-based art. Not being able to point to a bit of it and 'see' what we're talking about or 'see' all of the music at one time makes it very hard for children to talk about it at all. To describe music we have either to remember it or to try to talk while it's going on. This is possible but not very satisfactory. The section in this book on 'notating music' suggests ways of showing the music to help children grasp it more easily.

Teachers can help children to describe music by:
● helping them to focus their attention on the music itself;
● encouraging them to remember the music as it goes along;
● asking them to listen for and describe how one element at a time is used e.g. timbre, duration, pitch;
● targeting certain parts of the music e.g. the beginning, the end, 'the very loud bit in the middle'.

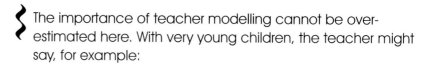 The importance of teacher modelling cannot be over-estimated here. With very young children, the teacher might say, for example:

'I heard the drum playing right at the beginning of the music. It went (demonstrate). It was playing a very steady beat just like this (demonstrate).
And then I heard the pipe playing as well.
The drum beat went on all the way through, even when the pipe joined in over the top. The pipe was playing very high up, with almost a squeaky sound. The drum sounded much lower and very hollow.
I'm trying to remember whether the pipe rhythm was the same as the drum one or different. I think it was mostly the same and just sometimes different.'

With older children, a bit more detail might be filled in:

'Here we go round the mulberry bush' has a very skippy

rhythm, hasn't it? Dumdidi dum di dum di dum – then what? Dum di dum again, and again. Shall we just clap the dum di dum pattern? It's long-short-long.

What about the melody of this song, the tune? Just sing me 'Here we go round' and stop – I want to listen to the tune again. Yes, it's all on one note at the beginning isn't it? Then 'round the mulberry bush' (sing it) climbs up a ladder and down again – like my hand, watch…(sing and show). The tune moves by jumps.

Some parts of the tune come back again later, don't they? Did you notice which parts? It was the 'Here we go round…' bit. Then, when we sing ' This is the way we…' can you hear how it's the same tune even though it's new words (hum tune without words)? We'd say it's the next verse of the song. Each verse has the same tune, but different words.'

Such examples show children the kind of thing that might be said to describe the music and introduce vocabulary to support description. To begin with, the children can listen and follow and fill in some of the gaps. They quickly make observations of their own to add into the picture that's building up. But they cannot learn how to describe music without being shown. Too often questions are asked but no examples are given of the kind of thing that would count as an answer.

There is a danger of underestimating children's abilities to describe music. This can arise if children's language limitations are confused with their ability to hear musical detail. Whilst obviously their language limits descriptions, once they become used to the idea of focusing on the music and describing it they learn the language very quickly. Some concepts are harder to grasp than others: concepts of pitch may come later than those of dynamics, for example. But children's ability to discriminate finely between one sound and another, and to latch onto what is going on in music in all sorts of detailed ways mustn't be overlooked. To ask 'is the music loud or quiet?' is not nearly challenging enough when children are aware of so many distinctions in between. Comparatives, such as quieter and louder, help to introduce more of the spectrum, but children can be encouraged to make all the much finer distinctions in between, so that their descriptions much more nearly mirror the feel of the music as it changes.

linking description to musical effect

A composer has to consider how the use of musical elements contributes to the overall musical impact of the piece. A group improvising play with particular aspects of the music's structure – rhythmic or melodic ideas perhaps – create the 'drama' of their music out of these. Performers make decisions about tempo, dynamics, and timbre which are based on their understanding of how choices about those elements will work in conjunction with the rhythmic or melodic patternings of the music to create the final effect on a listener. Making music always requires a bringing together of an understanding of the music's own structures with our musical response to the effect they create.

Children can be helped to develop their understanding of this process by talking about the effects created by music in relation to the elements which make it up. This is the 'so what?' question which follows the kind of musical description outlined above. As listeners, we can consider how composers' and performers' choices about how the music sounds link to the effect the music has on us. As composers and performers, we predict what effect our decisions will have on a listener.

Examples of this sort of talk are:
'the way the music slowed down there just for a second made you feel as if you didn't know what was coming next',

'the very high up sounds at the beginning made it sound scary, but it was even more scary when the drum did its low down sound'.

describing responses to music

Music has great power to draw responses from us. The ways in which we respond subjectively to music are enormously varied and changeable. Children respond as intensely to music as adults do and this responsiveness needs to be acknowledged and understood. Our responses are not all the same, however. Being clear about which are the subjective aspects of musical response enables teachers to differentiate for themselves and with children between subjective and objective ways of understanding music. Children's individual responses can then be validated by the recognition that we may all have different reactions to the same piece of music.

This is important because it is in children's emotional and imaginative responses to music that much of the energy in musical creativity lies. It is also important that children learn to focus and use these responses, not just as listeners but in how they perform or compose their own music. Several ways of talking about music can help children to do this.

talking about how music makes us feel

This is hard to do. The danger is that the talk falls into one or other of two rather stereotyped categories: 'it makes me sad' or 'it makes me happy' and stops there. It is not possible here to go into the difficulties of applying emotional labels to musical responses. If children are forthcoming, the teacher can encourage them to think hard and describe as nearly as possible just how this music really did feel today, whilst acknowledging how hard this is to do. If children are reluctant or find it difficult to say how they felt, it is much better to accept and respect this than to let the talk become a choice between token labellings, as above.

talking about what we like or dislike about the music

This opens up the area of personal taste. Just as we like different food or different colours, so we like different music. This is interesting, especially when we come to explore why. Why do some people like this music and some don't? Children can be asked to try to show someone else what they like or dislike about the music, to explain it. This helps the long process of developing independent tastes in music and again helps children become used to listening to their own responses when making choices about how the music will be made.

talking about any pictures and images the music conjures up

This is the most difficult ground of all, mainly because music is not essentially a representational art. It is also an area where different individuals experience music very differently. Some people almost always hear music as conjuring up pictures. Others never visualise anything at all when they listen. There is a more detailed discussion of this issue in the section on investigating music. In terms of developing ways of talking about music, this kind of talk works well as long as:

- it is kept clearly on subjective ground;
- it is not applied to all pieces of music as if all should have stories, pictures or extra-musical associations.

music through
movement

music in the early years

During the early years the child is coming to know the world in all its dimensions through movement; pummelling dough on a table one moment, running and jumping on outdoor play equipment, then trickling sand through fingers. The importance of action in relation to thinking has been well recognised in theories of how young children learn.

Music and movement are inseparable. We physically sense the movement in music and 'hear' the music silently made by movement. The qualities of timing, rhythmic patterning, phrasing and intensity are shared by both. So it makes sense to work with children in music and movement together both in musical terms and in terms of children's learning.

There are aspects of work in music and movement which overlap with dance: body technique, space awareness, a developing vocabulary of imaginative movements and learning to time and shape movements rhythmically. But for music learning purposes, the learning focus shifts to the musical sound, and movement becomes a means for engaging with music, for listening, understanding and for generating musical ideas. This is something more vital and demanding than, for example, adding some actions to a song or reaching high or low to follow pitch changes. Music through movement work might look as free in whole body movement as any dance work could be. Music learning exploits the movement abilities of young children and uses them for discovering music.

The following list describes the range of music and movement activity the early years child might be involved in:
- rhythmic movement play;
- joining in movement play with others;
- moving spontaneously in response to music;
- making actions to produce sound;
- learning movements for singing games;
- taking part in movement for music learning activities.

The teaching task is to foster, harness and build upon the child's own movement experiences and to extend these toward specific learning ends. This involves:
- noticing children's rhythmic movement play;
- guiding children's movement into music;

- introducing music for moving to;
- planning for focused music learning through movement;
- extending children's movement skills for music learning;
- providing resources for movement.

The relationship of movement to music needs thinking about carefully if teaching is to be based upon clear principles of practice. Movement to songs and recordings is encouraged in the early years but only a superficial understanding of the connection seems to underlie work of this kind. At its deepest level music-moving is a purely sensory experience for the child. Later it can be brought gradually to the surface as a tool to develop conceptual understanding. So, for example, the child aged 3 bounces instinctively in knees-bend style to the beat of the music heard but the 8-year-old can be asked to listen specifically for the rhythm pattern of the music and demonstrate awareness by matching movement to music. As a medium for understanding music, movement not only has the learning advantages of centring musical experience in the child's own physical self, it is also a 'time art', depending upon linear sequencing of events. As a time-space metaphor of the music it helps to fix what happens over time in the mind.

In the following list the possible learning connections are separated out:
- the qualities of movement and music are one and the same;
- movement is a metaphor for analysing musical elements;

For example:

silence	stillness	
qualities of sound	qualities of movement	Timbre
differences in volume	differences in energy	Dynamics
variety in speed	speed in travelling	Tempo
rhythm patterning	movement patterning	Duration
pulse	regularity of movement	

- moving to music is a way of listening;
  movement focuses listening and translates the music into a physical, visible form;

- movement and sound associations train musical skills;
  the rhythmic memory is developed through movement;

> ⌁ movement can be a source of musical ideas for active music –
> making, performing and composing;
>
> ⌁ there are some integrated music and dance forms, e.g. singing
> games and dance musics, which would not make sense as
> music or dance alone.

Taking part in music-moving experiences provides opportunities for
the child to develop:

- sharp, perceptive listening;
- concentration and memory;
- timing and rhythmic awareness;
- a balance of physical control and physical freedom;
- musical and social sensitivity.

And in music-moving, action, feeling and thinking are integrated
and learning is holistic. When children are engaged with every part
of their being an added sense of self-balance, of well-being and self-
worth are gained alongside the music learning.

noticing children's rhythmic movement play

All movement is rhythmically and dynamically shaped. So the child
playing freely is already developing understandings of pace, timing,
rhythmic patterning and intensity. The first stage in harnessing
children's movement for music learning is to learn to sense this
music in the free-play movement of children. Like all observation
tasks it takes concentration and an open receptivity to see what is
really happening. It may be helpful to stand back to look at first,
relax, concentrate:

> Two children had found a movement sequence which they
> acted out several times in exact unison. First they stomped
> around the corner of the climbing frame, their feet making a
> sound on the plastic mat, then they climbed up three rungs
> and jumped off exactly together.

A child played with the dough, rolling to and fro and then patting with both hands. The teacher joined in adding a chant: 'pat, pat, pat the dough' to coincide with the child's actions.

Just watching is often not enough. As with all physical activity we only really come to know it by acting it out ourselves. Partially imitating the child's movements or joining in by offering to partner rhythmic play will help the teacher to sense the timing, the energy and the rhythmic quality.

guiding children's movement into music

Children delight in rhythmic movement play with adults. In all cultures parents rock and bounce their young children to the accompaniment of songs and rhymes; to soothe or excite the child.

In the early years classroom little movement games can arise spontaneously from everyday moments. The teacher notices an opportunity, picks up the rhythmic emphasis of the child's movement and responds by joining in the movement or adding a vocal accompaniment. The voice is an excellent accompaniment to movement, instant and responsive to the smallest nuances. It takes a sharp and practised eye to watch the movement in order to sense accurately its movement qualities. As the two examples of children's voice play show (see p. 117), the child's voice play is often combined with movement as one. This synchronisation of the child's own movement with sounds, rhyming and singing, either their own or that added by another, is crucial in laying foundations for music learning.

In the beginning the child's own movement determines the musical input and not the other way around. Put simply, movement leads into music, not music leading into movement. Davies (1995) reinforces the importance of this:

"Children in the early years are busy establishing their own rhythms and most find it difficult to conform to highly structured patterns not of their own making".

Taking the child's own movement as the starting point may be a reversal of usual music teaching practices. Traditionally it is the teacher who introduces a set of fixed actions; these are to be imitated by the child to accompany a song or other music. The most obvious shortcoming is that this takes the adult's movement patterns as the model and not the child's own. The size of the adult in relation to the child immediately sets the pace and dynamics of the movements. Adjustment in this size-mismatch is expected of the child. The child must watch the teacher, imagine the movements, organise the left and right-sidedness, convert and re-enact and at the same time coordinate actions with music, perhaps even singing at the same time; very demanding for most young children until well experienced.

The two activities which follow model approaches in which the child's own movement guides the musical input. The first leads into a composing activity and the second into a song. Further ideas for working with the song are given so that the opportunity is not lost to allow one musical activity to flow into another.

activity

movement into music

➤ A thick gym mat is placed in the middle of a space suitable for movement.

The children run up to it one at a time and leap, landing on the mat in all kinds of different ways.

Each child creates an individual rhythmic movement pattern. The other children form a group of watchers and listeners, and are asked to pick out the sound of bare feet as each child runs up and lands.

Then the children repeat their actions but vocalise at the same time with syllables or words.

The teacher might watch intently and on a drum play the rhythm patterning created by the run up, leap and jump.

Now, standing still, the children one by one imagine the movement and vocalise their movement patterns.

They might go on to play 'run up and jumps' on different instruments and vary the landings. These can be listened to carefully, compared and the detail of the phrase shaping discussed.

The value of this activity is that it balances energy and èlan within the framework of a controlled activity; to run along a pathway and aim for the mat. It allows each child to find their own pace and patterning. The movement is sounded out as a musical phrase in voice or instrumental sound. Gradually sound takes over so that it becomes a musical idea which, if detached from its movement origins, still embodies the children's energy and forward drive. Movement in this way provides a substructure upon which our sense of rhythm is built.

When talking about the musical patterning with children the movement acts as a model for reference:
'did you hear the loud moment of landing?'
'this pattern runs up for a long way and lands softly;
can you play a slow run up and a very big jump?'

<table>
<tr><td>activity</td></tr>
</table>

movement into song

➳ Sit facing a partner, hold both hands and sway back and forth. The movements should tip the body comfortably back and forward just a little.

'With your partner find different swaying movements.'
The children may need some suggestions, to stand, sit or lie, perhaps to position themselves side by side, or back to back.

'Continue with your swaying and listen while I sing in time to your moving.'
Sing 'Way Haul Away' (see over) at a tempo which will match the children's swaying movements exactly. (It is usually a good idea to select one pair to watch and use as a tempo guide.)
Be alert to the differences in the children's tempo of movement and adjust the singing tempo accordingly.

'Stop your movement and listen to the singing. Just listen and hear your rocking movement in the song.'

'Now move again and the singing will stop. Just move and hear the song in your rocking movement.'

In this way the children come to experience sound tracking movement at exactly the same tempo. They feel and hear what it is to be 'in time'. Only then can the process be reversed and the child asked to follow the music, to keep in time with what they hear.

'Listen to my singing of the song now and "haul on the ropes" all keeping in time together.'

The easy swing of leaning forward and hauling back the rope emphasises the strong two-beat in a bar metre of the song and the dotted rhythm patterns.

watch and listen for

- each child's natural tempo;
- how they adjust their tempo to working with a partner, to the tempo of the song.

intervention

The teacher can support the children's learning by:
- modelling movements and joining in with children;
- describing the regularity of their movements and drawing attention to the matching tempo of movement and song using vocabulary such as 'in time' or 'the same speed as';
- suggesting alternative ways of moving (Metz, 1989);
- drawing attention to the strong/weak, 2 time metre.

English work song: Way Haul Away

Shanties were work songs whose purpose was to get the sailors to pull or to push together so that the job would go easier. Very often shanties would consist of whatever words floated into the lead singer's mind in the course of the job and might be lengthened or shortened according to the length of the job in hand (Lloyd, 1964).

| practise |

In the children's singing pay particular attention to the shape of the melody, the angular fall of the first phrase and then the final drop to the last note.

Listen carefully to the melody and practise singing the difficult twist of melody around the word 'bowlin'. This might be hard to pitch accurately because it is based on a less familiar set of notes (a mode, the mixolydian mode).

| go on to |

Choose lead singers to sing verses to their own improvised words. The rhythm can be fairly free, but then everyone joins the chorus and picks up the tempo again.

movement into music: composing

Children often make vocal sounds to accompany their own movement. This inclination to make a 'sound track' can be encouraged by asking children to vocalise or sing as they move. 'Dance-sounding' either by adding body percussion sounds which become part of the dance, or by wearing or carrying small rattling, jingling instruments creates a musical version from the movement impetus. At other times the music might arise from movement ideas; travelling rhythms, gesture shapes or dance formations. It then takes on a life of its own, the movement foundation sensed in the music but not danced 'out loud'.

The next set of activities show how movement can be a source of ideas for improvising and composing music:

| activities |

movement and music-making simultaneously

- Sing or make interesting voice sounds to go with your own walking, rocking, see-sawing, swaying, jumping, block-piling, sand sifting.

- Find an interesting way to go across the circle; sing, make voice sounds as you go, play your instrument as you go.

- Wear or carry instruments; with rattle anklets or bells (English morris bells, Indian ghungroo) find ways of travelling, run, walk, skip and listen to the sounds you make.

ꙭ Chain together some different ways of travelling to make feet-talking music e.g. sliding, stomping and skipping.

ꙭ Find some stamping feet patterns to accompany your song.
Now play your feet patterns at the same time with a hand-held rattle.

(see Kouralengay p. 123)

movement and music making together, then just the music

ꙭ Repeat the same kinds of activities, but now stop moving and continue the music. In this way the movement becomes internalised but continues to support the music-making. Alternate – sometimes move and sometimes play.

movement first and then play what you have moved

ꙭ Find a pattern of body percussion actions (claps, clicks, taps, etc.). Perform the movements.
Sing what you have moved, play what you have moved.

ꙭ Draw large shapes of letters or numbers in space.
Draw and sing the shape at the same time.
Just sing the movement shapes.
Join your singing-shape with someone else's.

with a partner, one moves and the other follows with music

ꙭ Play a follow my leader – one moves, the other plays.

introducing music for moving to

The first stage, starting with the child's movement contributions and carefully matching these to musical input, needs some time. Repetition and consolidation will bring the child to a level of awareness of the unison between their own movement and what they hear. This awareness will be emphasised by descriptive comments given by the teacher: *'now you are moving exactly in time with my singing'*.

This next section looks at starting with music for movement to follow. Young children are easily 'moved' into dance when they hear music. This might mislead us into thinking that matching the music in movement is easily achieved. But among the youngest children, moving freely to recorded music will probably only result in fleeting moments when they are re-enacting musical features. Much of the time they are having a wonderful time dancing but with little reference to the music.

Moving to music is a complex process of matching. First it demands attentive listening. Then features of the music must be perceived, selected and converted from sound into movement. And also the child needs a varied movement vocabulary for interpreting what they hear.

The sources of music for moving to are various and should not be limited to recorded music. Indeed recordings, although they bring a richness of music into the classroom, have the disadvantage of being the least flexible for moving to. A children's composed dance can be played a little faster for the group who are moving to it, the singing can gradually slow down, or the improvised voice sounds made by the voice group adapt instantly to the ideas of the moving group. Here, listed, are the various sources of music for moving to:

- ready-made songs, rhymes, raps;
- voice music improvised for moving to;
- children's composed music;
- music for instruments improvised for moving to;
- music played by others, live music or recorded.

Moving to music is one way of investigating. In this example, as before, the movement leads into other musical activity.

●———————————————————————————————

moving to recording music: Gending Kebyar Arini
[None such 7559 79204 2: track 2]

The gamelan is a set of tuned gongs and metallophones played by several people. In this Balinese style the music has a frenetic, nervous energy. Its abrupt contrasts of tempo, dynamics and texture seem to be unpredictable but are highly worked out. In Bali the music is used to accompany many kinds of dance.

| starting points | • before hearing the music do some movement preparation and warm-ups. Practise fast moving in many directions and sudden stops, all hopefully achieved without colliding; |

45

- sit and listen to the music for a first time – the children can 'scuttle' on the floor with their hands during the sound and keep them still in the silence;
- move freely with whole body movements to the music being sure to listen carefully in order to stop and start in quick response to the music.

| investigate |

- the quality of sound, the timbre, produced by the gamelan, how can this quality be translated into movement?
- the idea of fast movement and stillness in the music (the silences are not complete, some gongs can be heard faintly ringing on).

| go on to |

- explore metal sounds, their timbre and resonance;
- make some music for metal sounds in the same stop/start style, the music could be led by a single mover.

planning for focused music learning through movement

Teachers will plan to teach children specific aspects of music using movement as the learning medium. This section will deal with more formal aspects of rhythmic development, although an understanding of all the musical elements is well founded upon movement. Numbers, words, symbols and diagrams can support and consolidate learning but cannot substitute a movement foundation for rhythm.

| activities |

Sound and silence

⤳ noticing beginnings and endings:
*'Follow the sound of the maraca shaking.
Shake and stop!'*

Rhythm patterning

↝ making patterns and repeating:
'Make up a stamping, tapping, clapping pattern for me to echo.
Let's do it again, again and again.
Now echo my pattern.
Let's do them both, again and again.
Your pattern, my pattern, your turn and mine.'

Rhythm proportioning

↝ finding the beat, then going twice as fast and twice as slow:
'Swing gently to the beat of the song.
Now find a swinging speed which is exactly twice as fast.
Now find a swinging speed which is exactly twice as slow.'

'Listen again to the song.
Swing gently.
Find the twice as fast or twice as slow speed.'

Accents

↝ defining metre and beat cycles:
'Sing Way Haul Away and move to the song.
Stretch forward and pull back.'

'Feel the strong first beat and the weaker second beat.
Sit, tap knees and clap hands in a one/two pattern.'

Durations

↝ measuring out stretches of sound:
'Play some long notes on a cymbal for your partner to stretch
out to.'

'Find a way to measure the long notes.
Make up some music for movement which uses measured sounds.'

Phrasing and Form

↝ following the phrasing:
'Follow the phrasing of the song with arm movements.'

The above ideas offer opportunities for open-ended exploration of musical elements, but these same elements can also be found in simple musical repertoire, as the following example demonstrates. The teacher chooses an aspect to focus on, in this case, metre, phrasing and form.

British singing game: Sally Go Round the Sun

Movement, song and community come together in singing games.

This song was collected in this version in 1977 from children in Birmingham by Iona Opie as one of her collection of Singing Games (Opie 1985). It has appeared in many other collections of children's game songs gathered from around the British Isles, the earliest in 1898.

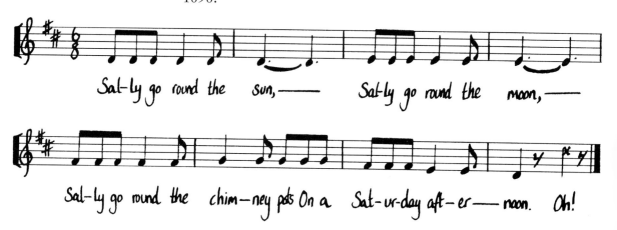

Opie describes the game, 'usually the circle romp around to the right singing the verse, kick their legs high in the air at the end, shouting "oh" or "whoops!" and then dance around in the opposite direction' (Opie, 1985:398).

practise	

- being one of a group;
- rotating in a small circle of 6-8 children (most singing games are played by small groups of friends);
- jumping and changing direction, well timed at the end of the song;
- walking or skipping in time (at first walking is easier);
- singing the song and moving simultaneously;
- timing the final 'whoop' with its jump, exactly at the end of the song. Then change direction and go back the other way.

investigate	

- the feel of the metre, the 6/8 skip which can also change to a bouncy walk and feel like two beats in a bar.

Sing the song for the children to move to, not as a group in a circle but moving independently. Find the walk which matches the beat of the song and then change to a skip. The children change when they choose between the two locomotor movements, feeling the difference.

---

exploring the sounds of instruments through movement

Movement can be one medium through which children explore qualities of sound and become imaginatively alert to instrumental timbre and dynamics.

- Play a drum for the children, eyes closed, to listen to:
  with the flat of the hand;
  with fingertips and knuckles;
  with a felt stick, with a wooden stick;
  by rubbing the surface with a palm;
  scratching with finger nails.

- Choose one of these ways of playing. Play continuously. Ask the children to find movements in response to the sound. Change to another sound.

- Play a cymbal for the children to listen to:
  long, resonating gong strikes with a soft beater;
  fast, finger flicks;
  stop the sound suddenly, crash and stop;
  one loud sound and wave the cymbal to and fro;
  zing the edge with a brush.

  And find movements in response to the sounds.

- Watch the movements found by some individual children and talk about them. Find descriptive words. Watch, listen and talk about how the sounds have been produced.

- Make up a sound and movement piece for one instrument with a partner. One plays and one moves.

watch and listen for
- how the child listens;
- how the child moves in response to the sounds – are the movements sensitive to the timbre and dynamics?

- does the force of the movements match the dynamics?
- the child's movement vocabulary and technique – are a variety of movements used? with control?
- how the child moves in space – the space around, in the room, in relation to others.

| intervention | It is likely the teacher will need to encourage the children to listen with concentrated attention to the detail of the different sounds. One difficulty with music movement work is that the movement experience is so direct for the child that it becomes the focus of their attention and they lose touch with the sound which is happening outside of themselves. The teacher should ensure the process of binding sound with movement is complete.

The work phase of the session will focus on encouraging imaginative and inventive movements and exploring the way in which movement qualities can be changed by the amount of force used.

extending children's movement skills for music learning

Extending the child's movement skills for music learning calls for sensitive guidance, the direct teaching of skills in a way which leaves room for the child's individuality and spontaneous contribution. None of the activities suggested in this section should become drill. Try to embed the skills in listening activities since uniting body awareness with heightened listening and responsiveness to music is a prime aim.

There are a number of movement skills to develop:
- control and coordination;
- awareness of space and of others;
- body awareness and movement vocabulary;
- timing and anticipation.

control and coordination

Developing children's physical control and coordination will be an important component of physical and dance education.

Dance-movement for music learning mainly calls for control and coordination of gross motor skills. Physical skills for making music with instruments and the voice call for control and coordination of fine motor skills. Of course the two are interconnected. Fine motor skills for handling instruments and for breathing and managing the voice in singing are supported by increased control of gross motor skills. A movement foundation of large and fine movements feeds into and supports all musical activity.

A simple helping strategy in teaching children fine movements for performance is to enlarge them and act them out in exaggerated form. If a two-handed drumming pattern is causing problems, practise with both arms swinging energetically in space. In a similar way Montessori recommended children draw letters in whole body movements before writing them tinily on the page.

awareness of space and of others

For the young child newly arrived in school, orientation to the spaces, the furniture and many other children, may take some time. Making formations with others, lining up, grouping on the carpet, sitting around a table, are common-place in the management of children in school. At first, children notice and relate spatially only to the children closest to them, the one in front and next to them, and have little sense of the whole formation. Many first singing games and activities are played in a ring and children will need to be helped step by step to position themselves in relation to others.

Any movement work which takes place in a large space must prepare the children to move with awareness to one another to avoid bumping or bunching.

body awareness and movement vocabulary

All movement work should be preceded by warming the body:
- the action of the feet and 'shock absorber' joints is important; e.g. bend and straighten the knees, bounce gently (Vanderspar);

- control of body weight in relation to gravity, e.g. lean one way and back, without stumbling over;
- awareness of tension and relaxation of the muscles, e.g. stiffen the limbs, then gradually loosen starting from the fingertips and toes;
- control of dynamic energy, e.g. experiment with different levels of force in rope pulling movements;
- knowledge of left and right, e.g. labelling the sides of the body.

timing and anticipation

When actions are well-timed, when sounds are well-placed so that the sound we hear is not a moment too soon or too late in the ongoing flow of the music, the experience is very satisfying. The ability to time well depends upon knowing what is about to come and being prepared. We can focus children's attention upon the preparatory movement, the knees-bend and readiness to jump, the pull back of the arm just before a throw, the 'getting ready' of the hand before a drum sound lands in the exact spot.

With the youngest children, learning to start and stop is the important first stage. This chant, or any like it, is useful for practising stopping and starting.

Up, up, up we jump together, up, up, up we jump and STOP!
clap, clap, clap...
step step step...

providing resources for movement

Ensuring children have enough space to move freely is important. If the floor surface allows, the children should go barefoot as this gives tactile contact with the floor and lightness-of-foot. In an early years setting one area may be set aside for dancing, with tapes or CDs which the children can self-select. Teachers can model, describe and suggest ways to extend children's movement.

Resources provided for music and movement which might be considered include:

- spaces suitable for moving, indoors and outdoors;
- floor surfaces, safe for bare feet and floor body work (or a roll-out square of flooring);
- large mirrors for children to watch themselves;
- good quality sound system and a library of CDs or cassettes for movement;
- scarves, pieces of cloth, stretch cloth, saris, hats and other props for movement;
- anklets and wristlets of seed pods, bells, long rattles to wear or carry e.g. magavhu (seed-pod anklets) from Zimbabwe, ghungroos (bells) from India;
- small, portable instruments such as tambourines, maracas, drums which can be held and played while moving at the same time;
- hoops, quoits, ropes and balls, to mark out positions on the floor or provide a stimulus for movement;
- puppets or dolls for imitating and interacting;
- mats, mattresses, sag-bags;
- video camera to record and replay movement, for children and teachers to watch and discuss;
- videos of dancing for children to watch, books, pictures of dancers representative of both sexes and many cultures.

assessment points

early stages

The child:
- responds to music with movement and can match movements to the overall mood, dynamic and tempo of the piece;
- can improvise movements for music work with freedom and imagination, using some variety of movement vocabulary;
- has some skills for music movement work: can stop and start with control, and move in space with awareness for others.

later stages

The child:
- responds to music in movement and can match movements to the musical elements of beat, tempo and dynamics;
- can improvise movements to lead a music composition which show awareness in movement of contrasts in dynamics, a sense of timing and phrasing;
- has a varied movement vocabulary for music/movement work which is used with control and coordination e.g. can coordinate a simple clapping pattern game with a partner.

early stages
in composing

music in the early years

Young children often have very rich musical imaginations. From the earliest age, children show musical behaviours which are creative as well as responsive. They readily make spontaneous vocalisations which take on patternings and shape and gradually come to have the characteristics of improvised songs. They incorporate musical patternings of sounds made by all kinds of body action (striking, shaking, tapping, stamping and so on) into play or movement of any kind. Sometimes these behaviours become the focus of interest in their own right and take over the child's attention while the sound features themselves are 'played with'. There is a stream of musical impulse in all this which can clearly lead towards musical invention, and later towards composition.

Working with young children's musical inventiveness, and bringing this into play whilst developing the skills and understanding needed for composing, requires skilled teaching. This is, however, very little different from other areas of the early years curriculum. The challenge is not on the musical front; it is the difficulty of understanding and recognising emergent work in its very early stages and of working from the child's perspective, which is so far from the adult's own. Not until children are nearing the end of the early years are they really able to begin composing in anything approaching an adult sense. As with writing development, teachers working with this age-group are laying groundwork, with most of the more identifiable results of it lying in the future, as if round a corner out of sight.

This section looks at just this compositional groundwork. It seems useful to take this as a topic in itself, not because pre-composition work with children is separable from other work in music, but because it perhaps needs some specific 'signposting'. Teachers have great expertise in looking at children's early language work and most are also familiar and at ease with the products of children's art. Music seems somehow to have been missed out in terms of its recognition as an avenue of children's creativity which has a validity of its own. This is largely because music as a performing art has taken precedence. The consequence is that for many teachers, parents and carers, the sound of children's music is unfamiliar, strange and unrecognised, we might even say unrecognisable. Since music does not have the directly representational function which much art and most writing has, there is no subject matter to bridge the gap between adult and child. We can't look at or read about the baby, say, and be engaged and entertained by the child's view of it. On the whole, teachers have only their experience of adult's music to compare with the music the children are making. And the differences sound greater than they are.

This is because the most significant difference between children's and adult's music is in the handling of the overall structure. There is a developmental factor in the ability to think of and produce whole pieces of music as opposed to a stream of music which is made as it is played or sung. From an adult perspective, composing involves the creation of a piece of music which is planned and formed as an entity. The music has shape and form, beginning and end, and its own dramatic course to run. To conceive of a piece of music in this way is conceptually quite hard, as is to grasp the idea of a structure in time.

During the early years, children can move a long way towards creating music which is composed in the above sense. A young child can produce spontaneous songs and streams of musical patterning, and becomes ready to some extent to plan and order these into musical structures which can be repeated along roughly the same lines on several occasions. However, it is only towards the end of this age-phase, and sometimes later, that children cross the compositional watershed which allows them to create music conceived of as something external to themselves and with a structure within its own time frame. This is a move from 'this is my music and I'm making it' to 'listen to this piece I've made – it goes like this'.

The adult who is listening to young children's work has therefore to make some major adaptations in order, literally, to tune in to the music children make. It is a matter of listening to the smaller scale patternings and hearing how they are woven together in the ongoing music. The concept of pattern is a central one. Musical patternings have their roots in very diverse aspects of human life. For example, they may derive from:
- intellectual, mathematical ideas;
- ideas generated by physical movement;
  a pattern of slides and strikes on a barred instrument;
  bongos played with the actions of a tabla player, using different parts of the hand;

*arranging a set of small instruments on the floor to give a
different range of striking pathways.*

● patterns of emotion and drama;
  *very intense, fast shaking of bells with a tight grip;
  rocking motion matched to zither strum.*

● patterns of spoken language;
  *'you can't watch the te – le – vi – sion A – NY – WAY'
  chanted and played simultaneously on a two-tone woodblock.*

● social patterns of interaction and communication.
  *suddenly finding a synchronised common beat with other
  children;
  picking up and copying from someone else.*

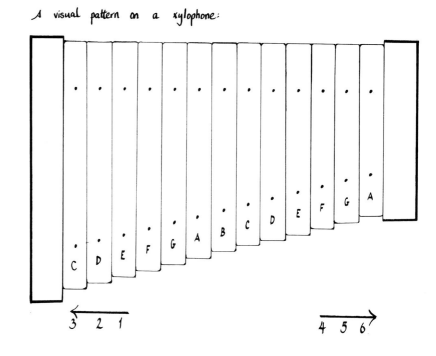

Adult composers differ widely in where the emphasis lies in their music. Children, for whom the divisions are very fluid move easily into musical patterning from any of these directions.

In the pre-compositional stage, the teacher has the important and difficult role of fostering children's musical creativity, whilst introducing the skills and understanding which will enable it to take shape and move forward. This cannot be a non-interventionist role; leaving children alone to get on with it is productive only in exceptional cases. But interventions need to come from a basis of de-centring towards the child's own musical outlook and teaching input made with the best match possible to this.

A further hazard is that children's priorities in the use of musical elements do not coincide with adult ones. This is particularly true in a culture where harmonised melody is a mainstay of much of the best known music, whether popular or classical. Just as colour and physical mark-making might be seen as foreground elements in children's painting, the quality of sound itself, its timbre, and rhythmic considerations are likely to be more to the fore in children's work than the dimensions of melody or harmony. This all adds up to something of a challenge until the listener becomes used to hearing children's music in its own terms. The challenge is worth meeting. Much of children's music has an energy, a vitality and a sensitivity which is every bit as compelling as its counterparts in art and language.

pre-composition opportunities

From an organisational point of view it is helpful to recognise the different kinds of opportunities offered in the early years classroom through which children can develop pre-compositional understanding and skills:

- ordinary play activity in which the child involves musical behaviours;
- child and teacher interacting musically, e.g. having musical 'conversations';
- play with a musical instrument;

- spontaneous song making, perhaps invited by the teacher;
- opportunities to plan music-making with the teacher and then carry it out;
- improvising music in a particular context, e.g. music with movement, music for an occasion, making music with others;
- trying out compositional 'building blocks' introduced by the teacher.

Each of these offer different kinds of musical opportunity and demand a different kind of role from the teacher. Some can be set up by the teacher; some occur as a natural extension of other activity. All can be planned for as part of the child's wider programme. If the teacher is clear about the learning potential in each and what it may lead towards, advantage can be taken as and when the opportunity arises. Through listening and discussion, the teacher can build extension activities which take the child's learning forward.

Some of these kinds of provision are introduced in this section; others are discussed elsewhere in the book in the sections covering movement and music with voices and instruments.

The teacher's role in relation to the above is comprised of combinations of the following:
- a listener who notices musical features of the child's work or play;
- a listener who reflects back to the child, in words or music, what s/he has heard;
- a partner in improvised music-making who interacts musically with the child;
- an informed observer who can make concepts explicit and connect what the child has done to other, related musical examples;
- a supplier of techniques, explanations and knowledge when they are needed;
- a modeller of compositional processes and understanding;
- an encourager of creative thought and exploration.

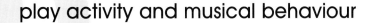

play activity and musical behaviour

As part of their play, children often run a vocal or verbal 'soundtrack'. This can fulfil any number of functions. It may simply mirror physical action – e.g. of pushing a car round a certain course, cornering bends, uphill etc.; it may be an absent-minded kind of accompaniment – 'dodidido do'; it may be commentary, or characters taking roles in a story. Young children move fluidly across the boundaries between vocalisation, speech and song; voicing their play can be kaleidoscopic in its use of sound and language, continually shifting as the activity engages them.

listen for	• rich exploration of vocal timbre and control of timbre and dynamics; • ideas which start off as rhythmic or melodic fragments and turn into more extended chant/song; • patterns which gradually change and develop.

There may also be occasions when children incorporate 'instrumental' musical patternings into play – where objects are tapped or banged together or scraped or shaken rhythmically or in a way which sequences different timbres or dynamics into musical fragments. Similar patternings may come out of dancing around, jumping up and down or doing any kind of repetitive activity . Any of this may be coordinated with the kind of vocalisation described above.

listen for	• rhythmic or timbre patterns which are repeated while a process of internalising the 'feel' of the pattern through body action takes over momentarily; • characteristic rhythmic groupings, the range of speeds of beats.

Notice the musical content of the child's play, even though from the child's perspective this is subsidiary to the focus of play activity. This can indicate the kind of intuitive musical 'vocabulary' a child currently has which can be picked up on or matched in games or other musical activities e.g. voice pitching work, action rhymes and songs, pattern making. Notice also how at times, the musical content takes over as a kind of emergent music.

the teacher's role

Mostly it may seem appropriate to notice but not intervene in these situations. Sometimes it can work to recall something to the children's attention later and take it a bit further e.g. *'when you were putting teddy to bed you were humming/making a song for him, something like....? perhaps we could make some of that song again now?'* or *'I heard all sorts of helicopter sounds earlier... can you remember any of them?'*. Some talk could follow about the songs or sounds themselves.

compositional learning potential

The child is engaged in spontaneous musical invention which is driven by an inner sense of purpose, musical or not; the feeling of inventing musically is there. Play can be the stimulus for widespread exploration of timbre, rhythm, pitch and dynamics, giving a context for producing and controlling sounds, vocally and instrumentally. Cause and effect begins to be established. Sometimes play leads to quite extended musical invention which becomes a focus in itself.

child and teacher interacting musically

Just as children learn much about using language through talking with adults, so they can learn musically through 'musicking' with an adult who will interact with them on a musical rather than a verbal level. An invitation, from child or teacher, of the 'let's make some music together on this drum' kind, or a spontaneous conversion of a conversation from speech to song, can open up many possibilities. A turn-taking framework with an instrument can lead to explorations focused on any musical elements, where both parties introduce new ideas, copy, extend or transform each other's material, or enter into dramatic roles or structures e.g. of argument, compliance, catching out, or humour. All these are fundamental musical processes and are also natural ways in which to interact with someone else.

Conversation implies a distinction of roles, where two identities are maintained and it isn't polite to interrupt. Musical turn-taking can move into a merger where the musical stream becomes a continuous one, with each contributor 'following-on-from'. Or it can use overlap and lead on to more of a 'joining in' format, where two collaborate, playing or singing together.

Making music with a child is invaluable for the child and it enables the teacher to gain insight into the child's musical thinking. Just as in the case of language, if the adult is skilful at adapting to the child's level of skill and understanding and is responsive to the feeling and 'meaning' content of what the child offers, children can gain enormously from having their ideas heard, responded to, reinforced, and referred on to an adult music–linguistic framework. Even at the simplest level of keeping a beat together, a young child gains the experience of what it feels like to keep steady, say, or gradually to increase volume or slow down against someone with greater control. There is also the opportunity to absorb a feel for judging the drama of the musical effect. The teacher can reflect back a child's idea simply by repeating it back as an entity, or can introduce new possibilities as part of the musical exchange.

| listen to |

- detail of the kind of patternings – timbral, rhythmic, melodic – being produced;
- musical ways in which the child connects with the adult partner.

Notice the extent to which the child is able to interact and in what kind of terms, musical or other. This activity can be an excellent way of communicating with a child who is reluctant to speak or who doesn't speak at all. Music offers an alternative way of making a relationship.

compositional learning potential

Music making of this kind makes an interface between adult and child understandings of musical structures and 'meanings'. The teacher can reflect back musical ideas to the child non-verbally and can help to 'scaffold' the music as it emerges. Such play also helps the child to build an understanding of musical structures which depend on more than one player or singer and which develop from musical interaction.

building blocks for compositional development

During the early years it is largely ineffective to try to teach compositional ideas in a direct relationship to asking for composed music in response. Older children are well able to follow an introductory session with the teacher, for example on how music can be structured by layering rhythms one over another, and then respond to a request to make pieces which use this technique. Their compositions once made can be brought back to another class session for discussion and new possibilities identified from there. This cyclical process is not so directly applicable to younger children.

The key difference is the need for a looser connection between, put simplistically, input and output. Young children's own music making is full of borrowings from all sources around them. A rich environment of musical experiences and possibilities makes an enormous difference and this is reflected in the quality of their musical work. But the links cannot be forced.

So the teacher can best contribute to enriching compositional development by an approach balanced between two strategies. One is by working from children's own music – listening to it, reflecting back, discussing, making connections to other music. The other is to provide 'building blocks' by introducing musical ideas, exploring them with the class or group together, and using vocabulary to describe in what is basically a 'showing and saying' process. The building blocks help to extend children's experience, to widen their range of aural images and to help them conceptualise musical structures. This is done by drawing on very precise 'single' ideas, introduced simply and vividly. There is, however, no expectation of immediate use in children's work, though this may occur. As the children gather more and more ideas so they will draw on these as their interest and opportunities offer a purpose for them. The building blocks become incorporated into the child's music making at the level and time which understanding allows.

The following is an example of a short session introducing one 'building block'. Teachers can easily invent their own choices of building blocks to match the interests and capabilities of the children in a group. Ideas for new ones often arise from other music in use in the classroom, for singing, listening or dancing to. Some additional suggestions are given below. The main thing is to focus on very small, clear ideas and yet to keep them somehow connected to a whole musical context. A ten-minute session at a time when the group can give attention and listen carefully is the ideal. The 'showing and saying' in this case is best if it is strongly teacher-led, at least to begin with. Go for impact and impression! Discussion and responses can follow later.

activity

building block: octaves

Use a xylophone (or glockenspiel, or zither – any instrument with a bar or string per note).

➤ Turn the instrument on its side, highest note at the top. Make sure all children can see.

'Close your eyes and listen:'
Play high C, low C, high C, low C, high C, low C, high C . Pause.
'Open your eyes. Watch and listen. Don't say anything.'
Play high C, low C, high C, low C, high C, low C, high C . Pause.
'Close your eyes and listen. Don't say anything.'
Play high C, low C, high C, low C, high C, low C, high C . Pause.

'Open your eyes. Watch and listen in your head.'
Without actually touching the notes, mime playing high C, low C, high C, low C, high C, low C, high C . Pause.

'Did you think the tune in your head? Did you hear... (play it again)?'
'Let's listen once more.'
Play high C, low C, high C, low C, high C, low C, high C . Pause.
'I'm playing high C, low C, high C, low C, high C, low C, high C.'

Next describe the pattern at whatever level is suitable e.g. *'it jumps up and down a long way...down, up , down, up'* etc.; or *' it's high, low, high, low...'*; or *'it's a tune for two Cs, a high one and a low one; it makes a very jumpy shape...'*; or *'it's two notes with the same name; a high and a low; we call the space between an octave, which means eight notes (count including both Cs)'*.

After the description, listen again.
'Can you sing "high, low," etc ?' (Use 'da da' or give words). Play and sing together.

Extensions:

'Close your eyes. Listen.'
Play high C , low C, F. (i.e. 'Hot Cross Buns')
'Open your eyes. Watch and listen. Don't say anything.'
Play high C , low C, F.
'Listen again.'
Play and sing high C , low C, F. ....'Hot Cross Buns'
Sing Hot Cross Buns together.

Make hand actions to follow the high – low pattern. Keep the pattern the same.
Play a catching out game making different patterns of the two notes.

Look at the space in between the notes. Listen to it played step by step. Sing with the playing.
Try voice jumps between the high and low. Try voice slides between the high and low.

Listen to the same pattern on another instrument.
Move the pattern to two Ds or two Fs etc.

Short is sweet here, but aim for as focused listening as possible. Eyes closed, eyes open, and thinking sound each focus attention in different ways. Saying it is different from showing it. Each strategy has its own purpose. Mix them as you need to.

The following are ideas for more 'building blocks':
- two-tone instruments e.g. two-tone wood block, bongos, a pair of maracas;
- suspended cymbal – 3 timbres with three different beaters;
- bell sounds – focus on duration and change of sound as the ringing dies out;
- pizzicato – different ways of playing plucking sounds on a range of instruments;
- steady beat using different timbres;
- moving up and down by step – on a barred instrument, a recorder or ocarina;
- two stick trick: playing in thirds, two notes with a third missed out in between, playing in 2nds;
- note sets: e.g. DFGA , EFBC...;
- moving a tune pattern in sequence, higher or lower by step or by jump; symmetries/reflections/retrogrades;

- trills;
- tango rhythm; or any other characteristic dance rhythm;
- alternating bass e.g.GDGD etc.

emergent music

These strands of activity and exploration are very divergent. As will be seen in later sections, children's earliest made music emerges from the whole range of musical activities. As with so much early years work, the teaching skill is to observe and catch the moment for intervention. Free-flow play leads into free-flow music and vice-versa. Brief, on the wing interactions with the teacher turn into equally fleeting musical moments. Becoming drawn into exploration of a single instrument leads to patternings which can be remembered and repeated. Asked for a song at the right moment, or busy playing in some other context, the child will make one, on the spot.

The need for a rich musical climate as an environment for early composing activity cannot be overemphasised. Children listen, absorb and remember musical fragments, ideas and images from the songs they sing, the music they listen to and play, and the music they hear other children making. Their own music draws on these and borrowings are a staple part of early improvisations and compositions.

As the teacher helps the child to notice the musical patterns in what they are making and reflects them back through verbal description, by singing or playing, or by representing the music visually in some way, the child gradually establishes the idea of music as a product of activity, just as a painting is. At this stage it becomes useful to start saving some of the children's work on tape. This opens up the possibility of playing it back for listening and discussion and the child begins to be able to recognise the music itself and notice things about it. From this point on, the child becomes more able to think in terms of the musical sound and to take control of it in improvising or composing.

investigating music

music in the early years

Listening to music and appraising it involves a wide range of skills as well as a readiness to be interested in the music and responsive to it. This section looks at ways of helping children to gain both skills and understanding through an approach which encourages a confident, open and enquiring attitude to music. Confidence is particularly important here: children need to learn to trust their ears, to ask questions and search for answers, and to use their own imaginations and responses as a means to understanding other people's music better. Above all, they need to become independent learners who can find and explore music for themselves.

Young children's attention is easily caught by hearing music; at a 'right' moment they respond with a natural interest and enjoyment. Children also quickly pick up and follow any musical responsiveness demonstrated by the teacher through facial expression and body movement, or perhaps through an intent and focused listening stillness. Partly this is a simple readiness to delight in, or be fascinated by, sound and sound structures in themselves, aesthetically. Partly it is an emerging, though still intuitive, sense of music as 'meaningful' and as something which is part of a shared cultural and social understanding in which they can join.

Taking an investigative approach to music listening is a good way to draw on children's already lively interest and to encourage them to be active in developing their understanding of music as listeners as well as makers. Encouraging children to bring together a curiosity about how music works and the contexts in which it is made with a willingness to listen, get caught up in it and enjoy new experiences lays a very positive foundation for all music learning.

Teachers can model this investigative approach to listening through the ways in which they introduce new music and explore it with children. This does not require extensive knowledge from the teacher, although knowledge is always valuable. Knowing how to find out is the key. If the teacher is clear about the range of ways in which music can be explored, skills can then be targeted and developed stage by stage within the wider context of musical experience.

choosing music to investigate

An investigative listening approach can be taken to music of any kind, encountered in any way. For example:

- songs sung together;
- recorded music brought into the classroom on audio or video tape;
- music used for dance, worship, or celebrations;
- music made live by visiting performers – parents, friends and others.

It is good for children to be able to hear music directly in context, or directly as performed live by themselves or others. This helps them begin to understand the very wide range of purposes music has within any society. Because of its roots in the wider culture, music of other times, places and contexts brings with it invaluable extra insights into the world. The class itself may be a rich resource for music: within a single group children and their families may be able to bring songs and music to listen to from a remarkable range of cultures, languages and musical styles. Simple music can give just as much scope for investigation as more complex music at this stage: nursery rhymes and children's songs make an excellent starting point.

Choosing music for children to listen to and investigate raises questions about what is or isn't suitable. Simplicity and complexity is just one dimension of this and is not at all straightforward. Much of the world's music is based on a single melodic line, either an unaccompanied vocal line or a solo instrument, perhaps accompanied by a drone or a drum beat. Such music can be infinitely complex in its use of melodic shape, scales and modes, rhythmic nuance and ornamentation. Conversely a complex texture of layered instruments may be essentially simple in its use of a single rhythmic or melodic pattern. Do children need music to be simple, and if so in what sense?

There is a whole literature of books written especially for reading to and with children. Why is there no parallel in music? The need for children's books springs partly from their limited experience of using language and partly from concerns about appropriate content, again related to the extent of their experience. Does music transcend limits of experience – either musical or 'life' experience? The answer to this seems to be that in some ways it does and others not. Whilst experience may alter considerably the way in which we hear music, there seems to be plenty of scope for making sense of almost any music at our own level and in our own ways. Children are no exception to this. Developmentally, evidence shows that children respond to the basic elements of music at different stages and this would appear to be tied up with other developmental pathways, in particular language learning. Moog (1976) for example, found that children's earliest responses are to timbre, and to words in conjunction with music, then, in sequence, to the elements of rhythm, pitch, form and, much later, harmony.

Music is often thought of as a universal language, though this is rather misleading. It may be possible to listen and respond to music of any time, place and culture, making some sense of it. But it is very hard to understand music which is beyond our cultural experience in the way that those making it understand it. We may even encounter music of another culture or a particular style (e.g. atonal music) which we find difficult to call music in our own terms. It is, however, much harder with music than with language to know when we are understanding it differently or misunderstanding it. And arguably, if it is still 'speaking' to us, we can still respond.

So it can be argued that children can relate to and enjoy any music in their own terms, as long as they can make some sense of it. The best indication of this is simply to try and see, since their level of interest and response quickly becomes evident. It is widely agreed that children should be introduced to music across the greatest possible range of times, places, cultures and styles. This is the basis assumed by this book.

Nevertheless, some guidelines can be given in selecting a repertoire of music for listening to and investigating with young children. Each of the following pointers highlights an aspect to be taken into account, not a rule to be applied at all times.

timbre is a foreground element in young children's response to music

Choose music which has vivid timbre (see p. 29); a single instrument, a particular voice timbre, two clearly contrasted instruments, a family of like timbres e.g. a consort of viols, a drumming group. Young children are particularly sensitive to timbre, often showing the ability to discriminate minutely between slight differences of timbre. This is an optimum time for the investigation of timbre and to link this to children's exploratory work with voices and instruments. Listen for the range of different timbres available from each instrument; simply contrasting a fiddle with a tambourine is not nearly challenging enough. Don't be afraid of a single instrument, playing a single line, alone e.g. a pipe playing a dance tune. Monitor the collection of music listened to so that it represents a wide range of instrumental and vocal timbres, singly and in combination, drawing these from a range of times, places, and cultures.

clear characteristics in the use of musical elements makes them easier to relate to

Choose music which presents clear melodic or rhythmic features; which has striking use of texture or tempo or dynamics (see p. 30–31). This might arise from a single characteristic throughout the music e.g. a dance rhythm, or from a use of contrast or gradual change. Don't expect these features to appear tidily and don't focus all attention on them; one element can never be separated in its effect from all the others. But recognise that some clarity in appearance of particular characteristics helps children latch on to them and makes it easier to describe and talk about them. Monitor the collection of music listened to so that it represents a wide range of aspects of each element. Has listening covered music of different tempi, different kinds of melodic shape and rhythmic character, different forms, different uses of dynamics and texture?

length of music is not a simple issue

Choose music on criteria other than length initially. Pre-school children can enjoy, memorise and recreate the entire 30–45 minute soundtrack of recordings they know, like and have listened to a lot. Equally, if their attention isn't caught, even a short piece may make no impact at all. Situation, time of day, mood and prevailing musical climate will all make a difference. Ideally whole pieces should be heard; to listen to extracts is like looking at the left hand top corner only of a picture. But it can work to spotlight certain sections and get to know them better. And it can work to 'serialise' as one might a story. All this depends on the individual piece however. It is best to make a judgement case by case. If using an extract, fade in and fade out to indicate that this is only part of the music and to let listeners move in and out of the music gently.

Notice children's reactions and try to encourage enthusiasm and interest by responding to these and not forging ahead with music which clearly is not getting a response. Balance this by preparing the way for new and different experiences – by modelling and by eliciting ideas from the children about what they'd like to hear instead. For example the teacher might say: *'That was very fast; I'd like to hear something much more calm and sleepy. I wonder if anyone could find something at home, or notice when they next hear some really sleepy music'*. Children can bring their own examples for everyone to listen to.

children's musical tastes are often much more open than adults': include a very wide range of repertoire

Choose music to cover a range of historical, geographical and cultural contexts, and also a range of musical styles within each of these. Children are open to all kinds of music and will often react in a much more positive way than adults. It is hard to predict what children will like and tastes will vary among the class. Teachers have the difficult job of trying to guard against introducing only the music they like into the classroom; unless their taste is extremely wide-ranging this is not a good enough basis for choice. Aim to foster the same attitude from children. 'Liking it' need never be a pre-requisite for getting interested in it. We can often enjoy saying of a picture, for example: 'that's horrible!' Why not? We shall never all agree. And there are many ways into different musics; our tastes vary over time as we come to like new things and 'go off' others.

children do not need stories and pictures in order to understand music

There is a small repertoire of music with story or pictorial associations which is often played to children on the grounds that the programmatic element gives them easy access to the music. The idea that music for children must be music with a title or story is completely misguided (Mahoney, 1997). It also leads to the exclusion of an enormous quantity of the world's music. The idea of associating music with literary or pictorial themes is a particularly 19th century European classical legacy. Examples of this might be

Beethoven's Pastoral Symphony, Berlioz' Symphony Fantastique, Mussorgsky's Pictures at an Exhibition, Tchaikovsky's Overture 1812. Paradoxically, the music itself in these cases can be quite hard for children to make sense of other than through the story, particularly if it is heavily scored orchestral music with complex textures and lengthy musical development. There is also a danger that the story ends up by standing in for the music as a kind of translation and as the focus of attention. Since music is not essentially or straightforwardly a representational art (Scruton, 1983), an overemphasis on such music can detract from a more direct understanding of the stuff itself. Children have no trouble in listening to music just as music.

approaches to investigating music

Just as we might consider how scientists do science in relation to how we approach it with young children, so we might think about how musicologists and ethnomusicologists carry out their musical investigations. This raises some issues which are not only interesting in themselves but relevant to how early years teachers work with children.

Academic musicology in its post-19th century form has been largely concerned with art music of the Western European tradition – the canon of musical 'masterpieces' and the work of 'great composers'. Its approaches have filtered down into the British school system through examinations at 18 and 16 plus, all originally governed by University Boards. There are strong traces still of these approaches to historical music study in many school music schemes at both secondary and primary level. One major element which persists is the choice of which music is studied. Many syllabuses used to limit the repertoire to music from 1600 to the present day. Since the rise in popularity of early music study this more readily extends to include medieval and renaissance music. But most school recording collections still reflect a heavily 18th and 19th century European bias, with a few reluctant excursions into the 20th century, now behind us. Additionally, there is a consensus canon of both 'good' music and 'great' composers, yet the criteria for what counts as 'good' or 'great' are not made at all explicit. All composers included in this canon are male; the history of the many female composers of previous times is not told. Larger scale, particularly orchestral, works predominate. Folk and popular music traditions are quite outside this. The reasons for all these features seem to be rooted in the history of music history itself and there isn't room to explore this here. But it is important to be aware of the influence of this practice, since there can be a direct conflict with principles of open access to a wide range of music and to a value system which is inclusive of the range of cultures, of different kinds of music – art, pop, traditional – and of the music of both men and women.

Another consequence of the above is that the methods of study of music are heavily influenced by the limited range of music studied. Musical terminology and approaches to music analysis have grown out of the demands of the particular and small range of European classical repertoire. A focus on the personal musical development of individual composers, of identified schools of musical style and thought, and on chronological sequence are emphasised, whilst social and geographical context are less important. When these methods are transferred to other kinds of music, for example folk music, popular music, music by women or music by children, they do not work so well. There is much current academic debate about exactly these issues.

Ethnomusicologists, on the other hand, have roots based more in anthropological study, where understanding the social context and cultural practice of music is the essence. Here any kind of music produced by people of a certain ethnic and cultural group might be studied and always in relation to the circumstances of its production. Whose music it is, which age, gender, class or occupation it belongs to is seen as important. Music analysis takes on different procedures too since one of the roles of an anthropologist is to make cross-cultural comparisons. This requires frameworks for studying music which are either culturally neutral (if this were possible) or sensitive to transfer across often very different musical theoretical and value systems.

It is useful for early years teachers to bear these perspectives in mind. We all come to music with certain culturally acquired mindsets about the kind of knowledge we have, or feel we should have, about it. The most useful starting point is an open attitude. In many ways, ethnomusicological approaches are far more amenable to use with young children than musicological ones. One reason for this is that they can handle any kind of music e.g. art, religious, popular and traditional music. The teacher can move across different musical styles whilst sustaining a consistent approach. Another is that at a very basic level, it is the social context of music which a very young child can most easily grasp.

Children can find out about:
- people who make music, who sing or play it, who compose it, who hand it on;
- the different occasions on which music might be sung, played or listened to;
- the reasons people have for making music;
- where and when music might be made;
- the range of voices, instruments and technology used for making music;

and begin to connect all this to:
- why the music is as it is.

ways of investigating music

Investigating music includes the activities of:
- listening and talking:
  getting to know the music;
  listening for and talking about music's patterns and structures, how it 'goes on';
  talking about individual responses to music;

- finding out:
  finding out about the context in which the music is made;
  using sources of information: people, books, pictures, objects, computers, notations;
  making sense of what we know: speculating, making connections;

- making connections:
  representing music;

moving to music;
making links with performing and composing.

These activities do not form a sequence. The teacher might draw on different activities for different pieces of music, choosing whatever starting point best fits the music. Investigating activities may become part of learning to sing a song, or a way of following up on music children have been making themselves. Investigating may go hand in hand with getting to know a new piece of music through listening to it; or it may be used to extend children's knowledge of music they have used for movement over a period of time.

Through this work children will be developing their ability to:
- listen carefully, to concentrate and give attention to the music;
- follow the music, noticing changes as they happen;
- remember what is heard;
- pick out particular aspects of how the music is constructed, based on the elements of music;
- hear musical pattern and form, understanding the music as a whole;
- respond to music and use words, representations and movement to clarify their response;
- find out about music by asking questions and using sources of information;
- understand music in relation to its purpose and context;
- use their knowledge about music to help make sense of it;
- use their understanding of music heard in relation to their own music making;
- enjoy discovering and investigating music which is new to them.

Investigating music is a thread which, like talking about music, can run through any kind of work in music. The following pages introduce some general and practical ideas for ways of carrying out some of the kind of activities identified in the first two groups above. The activities in the third group, on making connections, are discussed in more detail in the other, related sections of this book.

listening and talking

getting to know the music
If the music in question is recorded music, some thought must be

given to how it is to be introduced. Choose a time that will be right for the kind of listening you want to do and for the children's attention to be focused. Different times of day lend themselves to different kinds of listening. Other activities planned before and afterwards will also have a bearing on the suitability of the moment. Catching the right time can make all the difference. The music listened to will also affect the children's mood; take this into account too. Music can be an 'upper' or a 'downer' – it can excite the children or calm them.

Choose a place and situation that will help with the approach to listening you want to take. Children need to be gathered together and near you if you want to focus their listening and have a discussion. Different organisation will be needed for listening individually so that children will be able to become absorbed in their own responses, carried along by the music. It is also exciting to hear live music in its own situation: indoors or outdoors, in a larger or smaller space; and opportunities may arise for visits to hear music. Being an audience doesn't always mean sitting down: think of 'foyer concerts', buskers, or music with traditional dance. These situations can be re-created in school.

Opportunities for listening to recorded music might be:
- first thing in the morning as the class gathers on the carpet: *for sharp, analytical listening*;
- a few moments before or after a playtime: *for something lively or calming*;
- a small impromptu gathering to hear music which one of the children has just made;
- just before lunch to re-hear and enjoy a piece which is becoming familiar;
- time within a dance session or hall time for listening through movement or listening lying down;
- a 'work session' to listen and talk about the music and its context, perhaps linked to other topics;
- watching a video of music being performed: *this adds the dimension of seeing how and where it's done and by whom*;
- opportunity to 'choose and listen' on headphones in a music/language corner;
- listening to music instead of a story at home time; listening as to a story.

Think about different ways of introducing this music for the first time. Different approaches will influence the kind of listening attention children bring to the music. For example, we can listen with a feel for the impact and drama of music; we can follow it closely, trying to 'stick' to its surface and notice and feel the way it changes as it goes along; we can focus on one particular element and make this the foreground, e.g. melody, rhythm, timbre. We can launch our imagination about the music's performers or purpose or context and let this colour the way we hear it. Where we are seeing as well as hearing music our listening is affected by the visual dimension as well. The teacher can encourage a range of quality and kinds of listening by being aware of these factors.

> The following suggestions link ideas for introducing recorded music with possible learning outcomes:
>
> ～ *'Close your eyes and just listen.'* Hear the music; say what it was; leave discussion for next time apart from any spontaneous reactions children offer.
> *This targets the skills of giving attention to the music, being caught up in it.*
>
> ～ Listen once. Listen again with a suggested musical focus, e.g. *'listen to how the music builds up every time another instrument joins in'*. Show this visually in some way. Discuss and listen again.
> *This builds the skills of listening for something specific in the music.*
>
> ～ *'Follow the music with your hands.'* This is like hand dancing. It involves children in responding to the music's character and shape and the changes in this as the music unfolds.
> *This develops children's abilities to 'stay with' the music, following the ways it changes as it goes along.*
>
> ～ Children think of questions before listening starts. *'What questions could we ask to find out what the music will be like?'* This helps to generate interest and encourages children to find for themselves a focus for listening. It is an opportunity to build vocabulary and think about how we talk about music. Questions can be answered by the teacher before listening or by everyone afterwards.
> *These are the skills of thinking about how music can be and learning to ask questions.*

- *'I'll tell you one thing before we listen.'* Conversely, this allows the teacher to set a focus and to model one kind of musical description. Revisit the 'one thing' for discussion afterwards. *This is another way of learning to look for a particular feature and find where it is in the music.*

- Start with an artefact or picture – probably an instrument used in the music or a representation of a group of players. *'What do you notice?' 'How do you think the music will sound?' This introduces skills of finding and applying information and knowledge about context.*

- Start with a personal recommendation and introduction. Someone brings the music and talks a little bit about why they like it or why it interests them. This is a good way to involve new faces – other children (any age), parents, helpers, friends – and to find new music. It also models personal responsiveness and the interest we as individuals have in music. *Children gain understanding of how other people respond to music.*

- Start with exploratory work on connected materials or instruments e.g. wood and wood sounds. Children then listen to how another composer has used wood sounds to make music. *The skills here are of making connections, bringing children's own experiences into the listening process.*

- Dance first and then listen without moving. This allows whole body response which can be an excellent way of focusing listening and feeling the music. Notice that some children will dance while the music's playing rather than dance to the music. *This helps children connect what they draw from different ways of responding to music.*

look for	• ability to focus attention on the music, to concentrate on the sound;

- ability to focus attention on the music, to concentrate on the sound;
- musical involvement and responsiveness to what they're hearing;
- detailed reaction to particular aspects of the music, e.g. rhythm, timbre;
- understanding shown by language, movement, facial expression;
- interest in the music and knowing more about it.

Next, get to know the music really well, by listening lots of times and in different ways. As long as the choice of music receives a reasonably good first response, go on to give opportunities to become familiar with the piece. Listening which is 'one-off' can be enjoyable but doesn't really allow children to get inside the music and allow it to become part of their experience. In this way music is just like story and familiarity enhances enjoyment. Build up a class or group repertoire of 'music we know'. Individuals will have most favourite and least favourite pieces and this can be acknowledged.

If the music to be investigated is music made by the children, other strategies will come to the fore. Music sung as a group will be well-known to start with. It might be helpful nevertheless to tape-record a performance of it and listen together. The teacher might sing the song through for the children to listen to; or half the group can sing while the other half listens, swapping over so that everyone both sings and listens. With a smaller group, the teacher might bring a copy of the music and let the class sing and follow as the music is pointed to. Even if the teacher's music reading skills are not very good, this can still be an interesting way into investigating.

Music made up by a child or small group might also be tape-recorded and listened to as a first stage of investigating. If the whole class are looking at music made by a few, several hearings will be needed before they know it well enough to talk about it. This, of course, depends on the children being at a stage where they can re-create their music in roughly the same form each time. Or investigating might start the other way round with children 'interviewing' the composers before hearing the music.

listening for music's patterns and structures

Alongside the stage of getting to know the music comes the process of investigating how it is put together, how it works. We are all able to grasp musical patterns and structures as listeners, whether or not we have ever studied music formally. Helping children to notice what is going on in the music is a matter of teachers learning to trust their ears and having a simple vocabulary through which to describe what is heard (see pp. 29–31). Drawings and other representations (see pp. 101–106) can also be used to help capture musical ideas.

Once again we come up against the difficulties music poses as a time-based art when we want to examine it closely. We hear it and then it's gone; the music is always invisible so that it is impossible to point to particular parts of it when listening together. This is particularly hard when working with very young children who can memorise but are not so able to conceptualise structures in time. Strategies are therefore needed, first to recapture the small scale patterning of the music, and then to show how the larger structures and changes over time work to build the piece as a whole.

Strategies for finding and investigating patterns:

- Notice, and help children to notice, one or two particularly characteristic fragments of the music. These might be clear-cut patterns which recur or just e.g. an opening shape of a tune or a tiny rhythmic idea which turns up in different places.

- Be ready to catch these by recreating melody, rhythm and timbre patterns vocally to 'play' back to the children e.g. by humming or 'do-de-do-dooo'. These need only be sketches and children can be encouraged to use the same method themselves: *it's the bit that goes….*'. Listen again. Talk about how the pattern sounds, describing its musical features.

- Show one or more of the patterns found. Use visual 'notations' to capture some characteristics of these patterns. These could be hand gestures, drawings, patterns of stones, multi-link and so on. Listen and look. Use the notation to help to understand more about the pattern e.g. *the tune goes up and then down again; it's like an arch*'.

- Talk about the character of each pattern – is it smooth or spiky? how does it move? – in whatever vocabulary is most appropriate. If possible connect this to the effect of the part of the music which uses it. If it helps, give the pattern a name or tag: e.g. 'the wobbly bit', 'the dancy rhythm', 'the up and down tune'; Connect the fragment to its context. Listen and consider.

look for

children's ability to:

- identify, remember, and re-create or refer to patterns in the music;
- relate what is heard to patterns shown visually;
- use musical and other vocabulary to describe the music.

<table>
<tr><td>

progression

</td><td>

With more experienced children, the investigation can be extended to finding out how the larger structures in the music work. For example:

- Notice how the music is put together on the larger scale; listen for the shape of whole melodies, for repetitions, and for structures such as verse and chorus. As the musical time runs along what changes? What stays the same? How does the music keep going?
- Notice also the 'vertical' relationships in the music i.e. of things that happen at the same time. There may be a tune in the foreground and a drum pattern in the background; or different melody patterns happening together, perhaps higher and lower.
- Find ways of showing the plan or form of the music: with movements or by drawing, or by using objects or pathways on the floor. This is the process of mapping; but it's mapping sounds in time-space instead of objects in place space. Establish ways of 'reading' time e.g. from left to right, around a circle, along a line. Listen and look. Listen and follow. See how the smaller patternings (above) fit into the whole structure.
- Talk about the form of the music, how the music is built. This can be thought of as architecture – a structure built to a certain plan or shape; or as a drama – events with particular dynamic unfolding in time; or as a journey – on which we meet or revisit different things.

</td></tr>
</table>

look for

children's ability to:

- remember and think of the music as a whole;
- make sense of the ideas of musical structure;
- make connections between a visual plan and the music itself;
- use musical and other vocabulary to describe the structure of the music.

A little at a time is the key to this approach. There is no need to make heavy weather of analysing everything about each piece heard. Just learning to pick out small ideas soon enables children to start to make sense of musical structures for themselves.

 The class listened to a recording of Kathryn Tickell playing a tune called 'Da Slockit Light' on Northumbrian small pipes (Saydisc CD-SDL 343). They wondered why there was a funny noise going on all the time in the background. This led to discussion about the pipes themselves, a small version of bagpipes. A picture was needed to see that there is a bag for air with lots of different pipes attached to it. One pipe has finger holes like the recorder.

The children heard a main tune (played on the 'chanter') and the background noise coming from other pipes (a drone).

There was one pattern at the very beginning of the tune which the children could remember. It is a pattern of 'four notes, going up' (C E G C'). When the children tried to sing it they could tell it jumped from note to note. They listened again and counted on fingers every time they thought they heard this pattern. It came four times and then there was a long time when it didn't come at all, then four times more and another long gap. This helped the class to realise that the music is made of two main tunes, both repeated. Only the first one had 'our' pattern in it.

finding out about the context in which the music has been made

Children can be encouraged to think about and question how the music they're listening to came to be there. Investigating the context in which a particular piece has been handed on, made up, composed or performed helps children to understand the kind of thing music is and the variety of its uses and guises. For example, the backgrounds to songs such as the Ghanaian 'Sansa Kroma' (see p. 144), with its message about how relatives would care for a child if anything happened to its parents, and the English sea shanty 'Haul Away' (see p. 44), where the purpose is to coordinate the sailor's work rhythms, give quite different insights into how and why songs might be made.

These questions can be good starting points for investigating music:
- who makes it? *men, women, children, people in particular jobs?*
- for what purpose? *dancing, enjoying, to make us sleepy?*
- where? *indoors, outdoors, in the church/temple, at home?*
- at what time of day/year? *night time, work times, festivals, harvest?*
- with what? *voices, instruments, sticks and stones?*

They lead on to the questions of how the music's characteristics and structure are related to these things. For example, the pitch and melody shape will be related to who's making the music and with what; the dynamics and texture may be related to where it's made; the rhythm may be connected to its purpose; and so on. Often the answers to these questions are fairly evident or easy to come by; this is a valuable opportunity to introduce children to using a variety of sources for finding out.

sources of information

Children can be encouraged and taught to use sources of information for themselves. This can also be a joint enterprise with the teacher. While there may be occasions on which it is useful for teachers to tell children about music, there should also be plenty of opportunities for children to learn how to find out.

In the early stages, sources of information can include:
● people

Encourage children to think of questions they would like the answers to and to think who they could ask. Performers and composers (children or adults) will be able to answer some questions. Teachers as researchers will be able to answer others. Family members, visitors to the school and people involved with music in the community in any way, however small, can all be invaluable sources of information.

● visual representations

Children can use pictures, photographs, video (still and moving), reproductions of paintings, sculptures, ceramics, textiles, book illustrations, and so on as sources of information about music. Looking closely and interpreting what they see can open up all kinds of interesting avenues. Encourage children to think about whether the pictures are likely to be accurate or whether they come partly from someone's imagination? Encourage them to connect what they see to ideas of how the music sounds, or might sound if it could be heard. Try to use representations which avoid stereotypes; aim to balance race and gender across the range of musical roles.

● artefacts

These will mainly be instruments themselves, from which much can be learned by investigating closely. Again encourage speculation about music: about what sort of music the instrument would play best or what kind of music would be easy or hard to play on it.

Later, this can extend to:
● finding information from books or CD and tape covers
To begin with, share information found in this way with the children, making it clear how it has been found, e.g. *'let's look up…'* or *'it says here'…* or *'what we need is a book about…'.* This is just an extension of the kind of 'research' skills that are being built up across the curriculum. Later encourage children to look in books for themselves, for pictures and then words.

● using computers and CD ROMs
Where the school has such a facility available, it is an invaluable resource, since children can see pictures and hear sound at the same time. A gap is opening up fast between children who have computers at home and those that do not. For children who are already experienced, this can be an easier way of accessing information than books.

Children should be encouraged to feel confident about looking and finding and using sources of information about music as about anything else. They will quickly build up their experience of the kinds of questions that can be asked and of the ways in which music and musical contexts differ. This will gradually lay the groundwork for introducing ideas of time and place later.

making sense of what we know

It is very easy for the activities of finding out about music to become separated from listening to it. Perhaps we tend to 'listen and feel' as something different from 'knowing about' music. Yet how we hear music is partly dependent on how we think of it. Hearing music as a dance, for example, may make us hear it differently from just listening. In addition, knowledge about music gains its meaningfulness only in relation to the sound of music itself. In however simple a way, therefore, teachers can aid children's understanding of music by helping them to make connections between what they find out about a piece and how it sounds. Listening examples in other sections of this book illustrate this process in detail.

Knowing facts – for example that there are three players, that the music was written to be played at a banquet – adds a dimension to musical experience only if we try to make some sense of what we know. A middle stage of discussion is needed to encourage children to make this sense for themselves. Knowledge must be linked to the sound of the music. For example:

> *'If there are three players, who does what?'*
> *'If they all play at once, what will that sound like?'*
> *'Will they all play the same tune or different ones?'*
> *'If they all play at different times, how will that sound?'*
> *'Can we imagine what this banquet was like? Who was there? What was everyone doing? Who would be playing? Where? Who would be listening?'*
> *'What kind of music would you like to hear while you were eating a huge meal? Could it be any music or would it be a special kind?'*

This can then be followed through into listening to the music and reviewing the class's thoughts about it.

The role of speculation and imagination is crucial; listening to music involves imaginative thinking as an essential part of the process. This can apply to abstract music, with no very specific function, just as much as to music with the clear kind of context as above.

The process of becoming familiar with a range of music and enabling it to become a well known repertoire which can be revisited and enjoyed deserves some consideration in itself. Just as we tend to build our own personal collections of music we value and enjoy, so as a class or group a music collection of pieces that have been enjoyed and learnt about can be gathered. The teacher can use a number of different strategies to encourage this ongoing investigation and to help music newly introduced to become part of such a repertoire.

As a collection of familiar music begins to grow, consideration can be given to how it is kept and accessed by teachers and children as a class resource. Older children can be involved in this, helping to make decisions about how to keep and use recordings, where to display a list or book of items in the collection, and making their own choices of music for further group or individual listening.

Music can be sorted into categories and this can become a valuable learning experience in itself. Children can identify sorts of music and allocate new examples accordingly. Possible categories might be:

- music for voices
- music for instruments
- electronic music

- lively music
- sleepy music
- a mixture

- solo music
- small group music
- large group music

Tapes of children's own compositions and performances can be included in the collection if their music has reached the stage of being recorded and saved.

assessment points

early stages

The child:
- can give attention to and follow the music;
- can respond to music with interest and in a variety of ways;
- can pick out some aspects of the music and talk about them.

later stages

The child:
- can follow music, listening for particular features;
- can ask questions, notice features and talk about these and their own responses;
- is building knowledge of the contexts in which music is made and can relate music's characteristics to this.

notating

Earlier sections have looked at language and at movement as means for deepening and extending children's understanding of music. This section looks at other ways.

During the early years children will accumulate intuitive understandings of music by being involved in a wide range of active musical experiences. These ways of knowing are a vital source of musical imagination in children's spontaneous making of songs and instrumental music and in their movement responses to music. Hand-in-hand with teaching approaches which recognise the importance of not losing these qualities of spontaneity and playfulness as a source of creativity, the teacher will also wish to develop what Donaldson calls 'disembedded' thinking (Donaldson, 1978); that is, the ability to separate musical ideas from their context, to reflect on them, to talk about and work with them. Music is particularly difficult to get hold of, sound is invisible and intangible. To support the gradual process of bringing children to a level of more conscious understanding, music is translated into other media: gestures, visual symbols, syllables, words and notations. Once crystallised, musical ideas are more easily remembered, conceptualised, pondered, talked about and applied to new musical situations (Blenkin and Kelly, 1996). The visual pattern, the movement sensation, the syllables mouthed, all stay. This allows the child to stand back and reflect. All these translations are ways of notating music.

There is a further important stage beyond the capturing of sound in other forms. Having paused to look and learn more closely, the musical ideas which have been focused on and understood better should be released back into a real musical experience. So, for example, a song is sung and then one rhythm pattern focused on and investigated through all kinds of word patterns and visual symbols. The child should then be given the opportunity to use the new understanding, perhaps by re-singing the song with more rhythmic accuracy, playing an ostinato pattern or using that pattern to begin a composition.

The many ways in which music can be represented are listed, but bear in mind that any list artificially separates one thing from another. In reality these ways will all combine and interrelate:

orally

- oral syllables/ mnemonics;
  e.g. *'dum dum di dah', made up on the spot;*

- rhythm syllables to denote duration;
  e.g. *ta – te te (French time names);*

- rhythm syllables to denote duration and playing action;
  e.g. *pa ti pa ti pa ti pa po;*
  where 'pa' indicates tapping the axatse on the knee and 'ti' indicates tapping the axatse on the hand;

- syllables or short words to capture timbral changes;
  e.g. *gooong – ting ting;*

- syllables to denote pitch relationships.
  e.g. *do re mi – solfa syllables;*
  sa re ga ma pa dha ni sa – sargam, syllabic names used in Indian music.

visually

- objects;
  e.g. *pebbles, shells, threaded beads, blocks, plasticine, maths equipment (multilink cubes, Clixi, etc.) blocks;*

- drawn marks;
  signs, symbols, words, maps, diagrams with pencil on paper, on grids, squared papers, lined papers, easi-wipe pen on whiteboard;

- on-screen signs and symbols;
  e.g. *music programs for computer;*

- instruments – the visual structure of instruments; e.g. *barred instruments.*

physically

- gestures;
  e.g. *to indicate pitch, duration, timbre, dynamic etc.;*
  conducting gestures for taking part with others – signals for when to start, play, stop etc.;

- sequences and patterns of movement;
  e.g. *body percussion patterns to support rhythm learning;*

- movements in space.
  e.g. *to show the rise and fall of melody.*

tactually
- materials of different textures;
  e.g. *fabrics, papers, plastics;*

- one texture shaped into patterns to feel;
  e.g. *sandpaper shapes, braille notations;*

- vibrations – of the instruments themselves;
  e.g. *amplifiers, surrounding surfaces.*

Looking at the list and in the discussion which follows, the bias is towards ways of visualising music; this bias might have become the focus for the whole of this section. But symbolic forms in all media are included in order to remind us that there are many 'languages' of childhood (Edwards et al., 1995) and that music learning is multi-dimensional.

The use of many kinds of objects is suggested. This is the stuff of early years classrooms and is easily available and familiar. Many of the understandings of how children use these materials in exploring their learning can be applied to music. Playing with objects which can be arranged and rearranged is easier than with materials that mark permanently. For some learning purposes pen and paper can be too fixed, too final.

The emphasis on visual forms lays the foundations for notating music according to conventional systems. Using conventional notation isn't a separate skill suddenly introduced at a certain age but is one part of a continuum of learning to symbolise sounds for a range of musical purposes: purposes which are centred on the child's needs. The early years child should be considered to be at a stage of using notations in the broadest sense of which only one strand of activity will focus on conventional notation.

Many of the music learning ideas in this section have close links with the symbol systems which early years children are discovering in reading and in number work. It is all part of the first understandings that one thing can stand in for something else and once abstracted can do different things for you. Symbols enable the child to gain a kind of control over the materials, whether they be words, numbers or sounds of music. We should remember however that the child's prior experience of using language is rich and wide-ranging before they come to grapple with the symbols in reading and writing. Ideally we should aim for the same background of experience for music notating.

Some fundamentals, such as numberings, patterns and certain structures remain whatever their material, threading through unchanged (Athey, 1990). Three is three in movement, beads, syllables, marks on paper, whereas other elements, for example timbre, pitch, dynamics are netted by some media and lost by others. In other words, some elements are better represented by specific media. Timbre can be particularly well captured by colour, movement, by textured fabrics, by vocal sounds and syllables. For example, the drummers who play in the gamelan learn their patterns by vocalising the different qualities of drum timbre – 'doong dah tak tak'. There is always a danger that we focus too much on pitch and rhythm structures with children because conventional notation is a system for coding these very precisely.

two-way process

Symbolising music involves two different processes: musical sounds converted into representations and the reversal, starting with symbols and converting back into music. Each of the two processes offers different learning opportunities and the teacher must be sure to understand the musical thinking attached. It might be all too easy to encourage children to read back written rhythm symbols in rote fashion in a way which has very little to do with being musical.

To translate music into symbols, the sounds have to be listened to carefully, sorted, analysed and transformed into another media. The reverse process, to bring symbolic forms into life as music asks the child to interpret in sound, to imagine aurally in advance of hearing, to have musical ideas and make musical choices. And the opportunity to use and apply music knowledges already acquired – *'what kind of sound could we play for this sign, how long might this note be?'*

just a part or the whole

Children can be encouraged to look closely at one small part of the music, as if looking with a magnifying glass in science, or they can begin with the whole story. Small chunks and patterns can be isolated and held on to in other media, to be remembered and examined. These might be small patterns from a child's composition or from a piece of music which is being investigated. For example, to convert a melody/rhythm pattern from a song into a body percussion pattern holds it in the memory and etches the rhythm patterning. In this song:

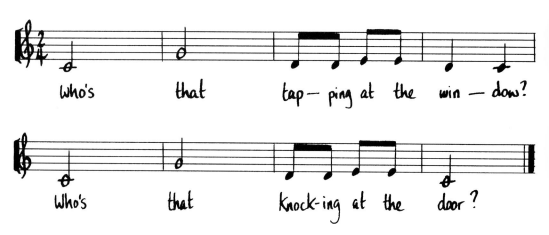

two rhythm patterns can be taken out and clapped and tapped:

> tap-ping at the win-dow
> 4 taps on knee 2 claps
>
> knock-ing at the door
> 4 taps on the knees 1 clap

Coming to know music in ever-increasing detail is less about listening to one element isolated from the whole and more about learning from comparisons. We can only really know about musical sounds in relationship to others; longer or shorter than this, higher or lower, smoother or rougher. And in the case of these two patterns, the differences and similarities between them. And then sing again to understand the place of these two music bricks in the song as a whole, that the first drives on and the second brings the song to a close.

To begin with the whole story of the music, from beginning to end, different methods are appropriate. Sticky paper shapes wending their way around the walls (Flash, 1990), stepping patterns which circle in space, ropes which curve and wind in pathways; all these are time-space trails converting musical time into space (Young, 1992). They use spatial thought to recall musical time and to map out the music as a series of events; kinds of music time-line. The trail tells a story in which the teacher can track back and forth. '*What happens in the song here where the rope runs straight up in a line?*' The story of the music can be retold in sequence, as a narrative form with beginning, middle, end, with repetitions and phrases which come back again or change.

Each of the sections which follow looks more closely at one aspect of notating with children.

listening, analysing and notating

A look first at starting with music as made, hearing it and converting into notations.

> A child has made a patterned piece of music for a drum by repeating a sequence of two taps and a scraped sound. The teacher asks, '*can you show me how your pattern goes with the red and green beads?*' The child lays down two red and one green bead in sequence. But how can the teacher know just by looking what exactly the child has in mind? – the child might be representing the different playing actions, the different parts of the drum tapped, the different qualities of sound produced.

The teacher encourages the child to explain why the pattern is as it is. This means taking on the child's perspective, seeing and hearing as the child does and doing so with sensitivity and powers of insight. It is often the case that gradually, something which might seem simple is uncovered to find a range of understandings.

To convert the sound pattern into a bead pattern the child must somehow stand outside and listen objectively; a process of thinking and analysis which is supported by being able to touch and move the objects.

look for

- one-to-one matching of sound with symbol;
- ordering of sounds: in a line? or other formation?
- sorting of sounds;
- does the pattern read left to right or some other direction?

notice

- how the visualised version relates to the sounding version, what musical dimension has been focused on?
- what the representation tells about the child's understanding?
- what this tells about the child's previous experience?
- what limitations it might reveal?

intervention

The adult's first move is to connect with what they think the child is doing. A knowledge of the thinking process used in creating the visual version becomes the basis for deciding what could come next: to consolidate, extend what the child has done or introduce something closely related but new? The teacher has choices:

- to consolidate the child's understanding, by touching the objects, replaying the pattern, allowing the child to look and hear again, now as a listener and watcher;
- to focus the child's attention on particular properties, e.g. the pitch of the sounds, the timbre, and describing in language to reinforce;
- to introduce a new dimension, to alter the objects to show something else, the dynamics, or pitch. Perhaps the child is asked now to listen and identify *what the pattern is showing now*.

In the example of work with one child described above, notice how the visual, aural and verbal layers all interact and support one another.

Children's first notating of music onto paper will probably extend from their making of music with instruments or voices. They may want to make jottings as part of the working process, create an aide-mémoire or write it for someone else to play. To find ways to write the music they must find ways to analyse it.

Here are descriptions (Bamberger, 1994 and Glynne-Jones, 1974) of the kinds of notations children might begin to use in their own work:

- the child may draw the instrument they play and include drawings of their hands or beaters;
  This reflects the child's initial focus on the activity of making the sound but there might be less analytical detail about the sounds themselves.
- different playing actions or vocalisations might be represented by various symbols, zig-zags or wavy lines for shaking or rattling, or for long voice sounds;
  This kind of notating is still activity based, but there is more focus on capturing the duration of sounds and different sound qualities.
- the child may make a series of marks, like tallies, to denote the number of strikes and perhaps spaces and gaps to give some indication of duration;
  The sounds are analysed in more detail, counted and measured so that rhythm can be detailed with increasing accuracy.
- numbers may be written and other maths symbols used (+ and x);
  'Borrowing' from maths helps to convey what is heard in the music accurately and efficiently.
- older children may write instructions;
  Writing skills enable children to document certain aspects of their playing.
- when making melodies on barred instruments, children often notice the letter names and use these to notate pitch.
  A wish to play longer strings of notes than can be held in the memory often creates a need to jot down note names.

Example 1. Jerome (4 years)

A drawing of a guiro and the stick used to play it. The random circles represent a number of scraping sounds.

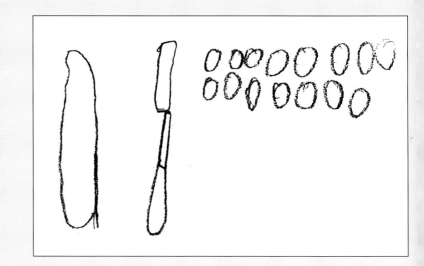

Example 2. Sophie (4 years)

A piece notated for a sequence of instruments played one after the other. The teacher has annotated the piece with names of instruments.

Example 3. Marcus (5 years)

A piece for tambourine and
guiro, notated with tally marks
and numbers.

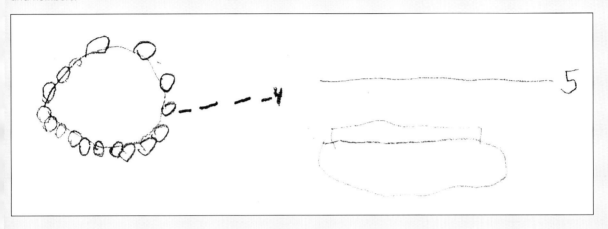

Example 4. Luke (6 years)

A notation which details
aspects of rhythm, duration
and dynamics.

Children's written versions of their music can be annotated and kept as part of a music profile, displayed in the classroom or posted in the music display area where parents look and read.

Talking carefully with the children about their scorings will give the teacher a window on their thinking. This may be the moment to introduce a way of notating for which the children have shown a need, perhaps a conventional way of notating rhythms, a repeat bar which could save a re-write of long sections or some of the signs for dynamics, accent, getting louder.

Having tried the process of scoring for themselves, the children will find it interesting to look at scores of other music. Ideally the children will have access to a number of different kinds of score. For visual interest alone they are fun to study, like puzzles and codes, full of intricate signs and symbols.

composing and notating

It is important to make a sharp distinction between using objects to visualise musical ideas as a support to the working process of composing, and using visualisations of music as a way of fixing and keeping a final version on paper. The two are very different things. This part will look at notating as one way of working with ideas in composing.

Early years settings are equipped with materials and all kinds of stuff which children can actively manipulate to extend their thinking and the having of ideas.

It is one small step on from working out how to show a pattern in red and green beads, to then reworking that pattern in its layout and sounding out the new version. Giving some kind of physical reality to sounds can be a valuable thinking tool in processes of composing, discovering, trying out, listening to and modifying musical ideas. Aural, manual and visual shaping work together.

Children's blockplay structures often have a kind of balance, harmony to them (Gura, 1996). Working with children using objects to shape musical ideas will tend to release the same search for balance and form. Both in objects and in music, small units or modules combine into more complex wholes where symmetry, pattern, repetition underlie as fundamental ways of structuring. However, it does depend on the material. Sticks, stones and dried leaves might produce quite different musical/visual structures.

As the children become more experienced, using objects can be a first way of laying advance plans, *'let's try out three of these in a line and then two more at the end here'.*

Older children might find the need to make jottings in a music notebook as part of the process of working out and fixing ideas. They may wish for graphic symbols which can carry more specific detail than objects alone. A small whiteboard and wipe-off pens allows for ideas to be tried out and altered. (Colours can add another dimension although notations are conventionally monochromic.)

symbols into sound

Earlier in this section it was suggested that the process of translating symbols into sound presents different challenges to the child than translating sound into symbols. To look at this even more closely, the degree of prescription in the symbols will also change the nature of the task. Processing some precise notated symbols into rhythmic patterns becomes a bit like reading. There is only one right way to 'say it'. It is skill practising. But thinking of ways to play abstract, drawn symbols of many shapes and colours calls on the musical imagination. It can allow the posing and testing of musical hypotheses, such as *'what might this bit sound like if... ?'* The symbols prompt ideas but room is left for flexible thinking.

The rhythm of pattern found in children's blockplay structures was noticed by Gura (1992) who added, "A sympathetic adult response might be initially to reflect this in rhythmic sound and gesture". Teachers might well spot opportunities to 'sing or play' patterns, combinations, shapes which arise in the course of play activity with a variety of media. They model and encourage children to convert patterns seen into patterns heard.

The teacher of a year 1 class plays with them the 'story of five'. With five multilinks she sets the children puzzles, arranging them in many different combinations of colour, spacing and layout, using three dimensions of space. The children choose an instrument from a selection and interpret the 'five', playing it a few times repetitively, for others to have a chance to listen and look. The listeners attempt to discover how the 'story of five' has been told and the interpretations are discussed.

With older children the aural imagination can be stretched further. They are given a song score to look at and asked to imagine how the song will sound.

Later the pitch shape of the song is laid out on the hall floor with quoits like a stepping-stone pathway:

The children must be sure to all sit in front of the pathway so that they see its layout. And as they learn to sing the song, individual children are invited to 'step the path'. There is something very memorable about using your whole body in this way and rules of *'only stepping at the right moment and in the right order'* seem to take the interest of every child. The aim of such work is to encourage children to aurally imagine in advance of hearing the music out loud. To imagine sound internally is one of the fundamental music skills.

environmental notation

Just as teachers support language learning by providing a rich environment for literacy, so they can equip the nursery or classroom for music literacy.

They might provide:
- songbooks and music scores in the book area;
- poster-sized notations of known songs on the wall;
- graphic notations of pieces of music which the children are listening to at story times;
- displays of children's music in notation;
- notations discovered by exploring CD ROM;
- books about music;
- computer programs with symbols and notations;
- large-scale grids and lines for 'emergent' music writing.

During the early years children are discovering that all kinds of visually intriguing marks can carry messages. This is the time to find out that they can also carry music messages.

Teachers using music copies, being interested in them, always showing the way the song or music played has been written (or not written but remembered aurally), keeping and displaying notations, are all part of modelling behaviour which is well familiar to early years teachers in creating a literate classroom. In such ways children are orientated to music literacy.

Children enjoy 'reading' music-notated texts for music which they already know well. It gives them a chance to begin to puzzle for themselves how music literacy works and to get a first grip on the systems.

introducing pre-notations

All the ways of translating music into less abstract forms, visualising, verbalising and moving it, will form the basis of learning to use conventional notations. Teachers will wish to expand children's growing competence with using symbolic forms and bring it alongside the first stages of introducing notations. Looked at in one way, notations are just coding systems which can be broken down into small logical learning steps. These might be called 'pre-notations'.

A useful parallel can be made with maths teaching. First measuring is carried out with everyday objects to establish certain principles of measurement, but then the need for conventions and some uniformity arises and standard units of measurement are introduced. There is not a sharp line between informal and conventional forms of notating (or measuring), but a growing need for formality for certain musical purposes. Precision enables ideas to be carried accurately, for storing music or giving to others to play.

At the same time children should be encouraged to keep all forms of notating running; one doesn't supersede the other. Ideally children will have at their disposal a range of notations from which they choose and an awareness of the different purposes for which they might be best used.

Children are learning and using mark-making in a range of contexts. They make lines, blobs, circles and so on, and place them on lines and grids in maths, science, technology. Notating can be a bit like data handling, both graphically with the number of linear directions (horizontal, vertical and diagonal) and in the sense of converting sound data into symbols which carry measurable information.

In pre-notations, rhythm and pitch are usually separated and learnt independently. In standard staff notation, rhythm occupies horizontal space on a page and spacing can represent different durations.

Here is the pattern from the earlier song represented in a kind of names and stem notation in which the 'blobs' have been left off. This is a method of pre-notation used in the approach known as the Kodaly method. This makes them cleaner for the eye and quicker and neater to write. Using only the two notes, $|$ and $\sqcap$ which is twice as fast (or two half-beats) it is possible to make a wide variety of patterns. The introduction of the note $\llcorner$ for twice as slow, or a measure of two beats, increases possibilities further.

To return to one of the songs used earlier.

It becomes:

The purpose here is to provide a glimpse at some pre-notation approaches which teachers might like to research further and to refer to resources which would provide detailed information (Forrai, 1974; Hanke, 1994; Stocks and Maddocks, 1992).

In staff notation, pitch occupies vertical space. Gestures which indicate for the children, particularly when singing, the relative pitch shapes of the melody are helpful for developing pitch accuracy (see 'music for voice' pp. 132–3). Gym ladders in the hall are often good pitch notators, particularly if children must climb up and down them. They introduce the idea of a vertical grid for pitch notation. Children's first attempts to 'draw' each sound of the melody on paper and to show where it rises and falls can be surprisingly accurate (plus the pleasure of creating rows of tightly rotational blobs).

Two first steps seem to be crucial in introducing pitch notation. The first is that young children need to get their 'eye' in so that they can perceive the separate lines and locate notes on different parts of the stave. A lot of quick looking-games are needed. The second is the understanding that the sequence of notes moves from space, to line, to space – and so on. Very often children draw notes at first in all the spaces or on all the lines.

Children's first attempts with pre-notations are likely to be highly supported, with teachers working closely with the children to prompt and assist, just as with all early readers.

And finally, a caution, that notating should always serve a musical learning purpose and in some way enable children to make and take part in musical experiences more responsively and imaginatively – and not become a learning goal in itself.

assessment points

early stages

The child:
- can make and understand connections between simple notations and musical sounds.

later stages

The child:
- can make and understand connections between notations and musical sounds in relation to each musical element.

music for voice

From earliest days young children use their voices with great versatility and expressive power. First babblings and cooings give way to playing with sounds and newly learnt words, making dramatic voice sounds as part of play and private sing-talking. Children discover the varieties of sound possible with the voice and are learning to use these to communicate, not just through speech but through all the vocal sounds, the small inflexions, the timings and changes in dynamic which run alongside speech.

So the young child arrives at school already practised at making voice-music. For the teacher here, in voice play, is a ready made starting point for making music with voices upon which to build. But one which is perhaps overlooked, and the teaching of standard songs, to quite large groups of children, very often comes to dominate in the early years of schooling. Singing is one important strand of musical experience but it is valuable to think of music with the voice in broader terms as a network of many kinds of vocal activity. This is, after all, in keeping with the way young children themselves use the voice. Indeed, learning to sing taught songs might be seen as an endpoint, something to aim for in early years music, rather than a starting point. Children arrive in school sometimes with very little prior experience of singing and will need much preparatory work in finding their voices and learning to pitch them. Varied vocal activity, spontaneous song singing, voice play and teacher-led games provide such opportunities for finding voice freedoms and practising.

The following list introduces the range of ways children might be involved in making music with the voice in early years schooling:
- voice play;
- joining in rhymes or songs;
- playing with words, rhyming;
- improvising and composing chants and songs;
- learning to sing songs;
- learning voice skills.

Where to start? First by discovering what children's voice play and spontaneous singing sounds like; listening.

voice play

Taking time to observe children at play in an early years setting will reveal a wealth of voice play. Here are two observations and listenings transcribed from video recordings:

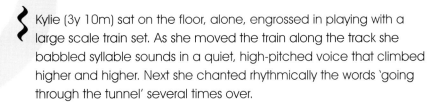

> Kylie (3y 10m) sat on the floor, alone, engrossed in playing with a large scale train set. As she moved the train along the track she babbled syllable sounds in a quiet, high-pitched voice that climbed higher and higher. Next she chanted rhythmically the words 'going through the tunnel' several times over.

> James (4y 2mo) played on the climbing frame outside, jumping up and down on the top platform. He called to a nursery worker, 'you can't get me!' chanting on two notes. The teacher replied, matching the child's call with a sung response. The calling back and forth continued for several turns. James became increasingly excited by the game.

In these examples, and many others like them, the teacher might notice children playing with word sounds and syllables, a continuation from babyhood babbling. Children sing-talk to themselves or make up on-the-spot chants which they sing repeatedly. The child's voice play seems to be closely connected with movement; either the child's own physical movement as he jumped up and down or the movement of a toy being sung along the track. It would be difficult to separate out the vocal play from the whole activity; the moving, the thinking and feeling.

Notice the roles taken by the teachers in each example. To have intervened and joined with Kylie's solitary train play would have intruded. The teacher stood back, watched, listened and recorded the moment. In James' case he was calling to the adult who joined in the game creating a spontaneous call and response sequence with him. In both examples the intervention was carefully matched in response to the child's contribution.

The child's interest in spontaneous singing will be sustained by verbal and non-verbal responses of the teachers around. Eye-contact, facial expression and gesture adds to the special quality of listening to children. A comment will acknowledge that the voice activity has been listened to and can describe back, helping the child to become aware on a different level of their own voice play and how it has sounded to others.

In research carried out by Tarnowski (1994) she explored the effects of different styles of teacher intervention upon the voice play of young children in a nursery. Those children who had been supported by an 'observer' who was attentive and provided verbal feedback but no form of direct instruction later showed much more variety and inventiveness in their voice play than other groups whose teachers had adopted a more directive role.

joining in with rhymes and songs

The teacher may initiate vocal play by playing voice games, improvising song play or singing known songs with and for children. This might be spontaneous on the part of the teacher, to capture a moment or to accompany a routine, or it might be part of the planned day, to sit on the carpet for singing with a songbook just as one might be available for story reading. Puppet play in which the puppet sing-plays with the child (see p. 125) can be particularly successful in encouraging young children to find their singing voices (Suthers, 1996).

The youngest children are probably not ready to take part in formal group singing experiences but will cluster around anyone who looks ready to play. The teacher models singing and other voice play for the child and provides opportunities for them to listen attentively and take part in whatever way they are able. Children often begin by joining in with just a fragment of the rhyme or song and by taking part in game actions and rhythmic movements. Taking part is the essence so that singing is primarily a sociable experience.

This one-to-one interaction between teacher and child enables the teacher to notice and build upon the child's contribution, introducing small step by step challenges in a playful but guided situation.

The teacher might observe whether the child can:
- listen attentively;
- respond with eye contact and facial expression;
- produce a range of vocal sounds;
- find their singing voice;
- join in with fragments of the song or rhyme;
- take part in game actions or rhythmic movement.

one-liners

Many first 'joining in with' songs are chant-like one-liners which sit somewhere on the borderline between speech and song. Teachers may make such songs out of often repeated classroom instructions (Flash, 1990) such as *'clearing-up time!'* or *'come and sit on the carpet'*. In this way small songs emerge from and become part of the fabric of daily classroom life.

Here are four songs for first singing:

Hop tu — nay   Hop tu — nay

(whispered) Jinny she jumped right over the house to catch the mouse

Hop tu — nay   Hop tu — nay.

Star light, star bright, first star I see to-night.

Wish I may, wish I might, have the wish I wish to-night.

joining-in song: Bluebells, Cockle Shells

Childhood has its own songs, baby and toddler lullabies, bouncing games, jig-jog ditties and tickling rhymes; songs which are sung by adults for young children to take part in. Older children out playing have traditionally had their own singing games. This is an English skipping game in which the challenge is to see who can do the most 'stitches' or skips. The game is adapted for teachers to sing for and with the youngest children to encourage them to take part.

Blue — bells, cock-le shells, Ee — vie — - i — vie — o — ver, I — van's in the kitch — en Do — ing a bit of stitch — ing, How man — y stitch — es did he do? One stitch, Two Stitch, three...

Hold both hands with a partner. (Teachers should offer children just one finger for clasping so that the child can release the grasp when they wish.) Swing both arms gently from side to side in time to the song. When it comes to 'stitching' mark out the counting with a downward bounce of both hands. The children decide how many stitches to count out each time. Children will have their own names for their primary carers, substitute these for each child in turn.

listen and watch for

- each child's response to joining in with others;
- how each child joins in with voice (or not);
- how each child moves, level of coordination and control.

notice

- if joining in with singing, how their voice pitching matches the song;
- if joining in with movement, whether the child is swinging to a regular tempo.

| intervention |

In this song the teacher might partner children in turn and adjust the singing each time to the new child's contribution. Careful observation will tell the teacher just what support the child needs.

| progression |

When children are able to join in with singing confidently new challenges are set:
- changing the pitch of the song, higher or lower;
- the tempo of the arm sway is changed and the singing becomes faster/slower;
- the dynamics are varied, sung quietly, louder or with variations of dynamics.

playing with words and rhyming

There is music in language. Creating an early years environment rich in rhymes, poems, chants, riddles and word games, drawn from a range of oral traditions, is not only valuable for laying the foundations of language learning (Whitehead, 1996) but for music also.

Patterns of words can be taken from songs and spoken rhythmically. For example:

> *eevie ivie*
> *eevie ivie*
> *eevie ivie*
> *over –*

– perhaps repeated in sequence and said with many different voices, whispering, shouting, growling, squeaking and so on. Opportunities to discover and try out different voices are important for developing vocal freedom and variety. The one-liner chant (see above) 'Hop tu nay' combines singing with whispering and requires the children to change quickly from one to the other. Children can be encouraged to play around with their voices, '*Can you wobble it, stretch it, twang it, slide it?*' (Victor-Smith, 1996).

Rhyming activities offer opportunities to explore the musical elements; where the accents fall, steady beat and metre, rhythm patterning and silences. For example, this well-known rhyme:

> *One potato*
> *two potato*
> *three potato*
> *four –*
> *five potato*
> *six potato*
> *seven potato*
> *MORE! –*

– has a skipping rhythm throughout but a silence after 'four' and 'more'. The repetition builds towards the climax on MORE! The rhyme can get louder and louder, or start loud and become much quieter and end with a surprise shout and clap on the MORE! The possibilities for variation with such simple materials are endless. The inventiveness will come from the children who can be given the opportunity to offer their own versions.

The next chanting game is more suitable for older children. The rhyme has a vigorous, syncopated rhythm to it which is picked up in the strong consonants of the words 'Kourilengay, Kalengena'.

● ───────────────────────────────

children's chanting game from Tanzania: Kourilengay Kalengena

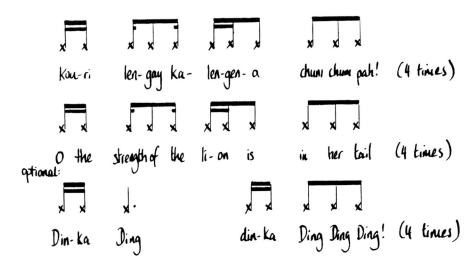

The children process, conga style, and stamp three times on the 'chum chum pah!'. Think of dance in the African way, that the dancer is a drummer with the ground for a drum.

Children then stand and chant rhythmically the phrase 'O the strength of the lion etc.' and one child improvises a lion dance.

Different animals are chosen for the next verses and where the strength lies must be decided. (Be sure to alternate gender for animals.)

The chant 'dinka ding' is a kind of vocal percussion and should be spoken with lively rhythm and clear diction. These are the word sounds given in the rhyme, but the children could invent their own vocal percussion from short rhythmic sound words.

improvising and composing

Young children readily make up their own songs as part of all kinds of play. In the early years the differentiation between song and speech is hardly marked. Later children gradually separate out the two kinds of voice use and singing becomes limited to a particular and intentional kind of activity. Unfortunately, teachers often reinforce this separation earlier than necessary, sometimes even discouraging singing either directly as 'being noisy' or indirectly by negative attitudes or modelling. The initial readiness children have to use song as a quite normal medium of expression can be built on as a basis for improvising and composing songs.

Composing with the voice has the substantial advantage that children can tap directly into their musical sense, without the difficulty of managing to control sound produced externally on an instrument. In most cases they also have substantial direct experience of hearing and singing songs, which is not paralleled in instrumental music. The connection of language use and vocal music adds a further dimension at a stage when children are particularly sensitive to the intonation and rhythms of speech. As a result of all this, children's early song compositions are usually much more advanced musically than their instrumental pieces (Glover, 1993).

spontaneous song making

Coral Davies (1986) notes how a spontaneous song sung by a 3-year-old reveals 'how much music she has already absorbed from her experience in the nursery and at home'. Children's songs draw on aspects of song structure and styles of singing they've heard, as well as fragments of songs known to them. Hargreaves (1986) discusses research by Moog, McKernon and others into children's early song making which identifies among other things a 'pot-pourri' element as children incorporate elements of known songs into their own song making.

song making opportunities

The question '*Would anyone like to sing us a song?*' usually produces lots of volunteers who will readily stand up and sing to the group. Some of the songs offered will be solo versions of known songs, probably from the class repertoire. Others will be new inventions. Often in the early stages these are narrative songs telling a story in a part singing, part chanting style. The difference between performing an already-made song and making one up can be discussed and gradually clarified until the more focused question '*Would anyone like to **make** us a song?*' is understood as a request for an improvisation. These spontaneous songs have a value of their own as well as being a springboard for the more composed pieces which follow.

Songs can be 'commissioned' to go with stories that are being read together. A story character might sing a song; words of a story (e.g. the kind of repetitive phrases often found in stories for young children) might be set to a small fragment of tune; songs can be included as part of a dramatisation of a well known book. Hand puppets can be used either to encourage single songs e.g. '*what is Zebedee singing?*' or for a child to hold improvised singing conversations with the teacher or another child.

Songs can be made up to accompany activities that form part of the ritual of the day: these might be 'good morning' songs, lining-up or tidying-up songs, putting-on-coats songs or ready-for-home songs. Or particular occasions such as birthdays or goodbyes might merit a new song. This kind of song might be made up and learnt by a group, helped by the teacher, or one child could suggest words and a tune which everyone could learn.

For older children, almost any kind of writing opportunity can be extended into song making – a song to go with a picture, to tell of a special event, to describe a pet, a song instead of a poem, Teddy's song, and so on.

The teacher's role is first and foremost to encourage and to be a listener.

Many children will make songs on the spot with words and tune arriving together. In the early stages, and if the song is clear-cut and fairly simple, the teacher can help by remembering the song and singing it back or helping the child to sing it again and 'learn' it. This aids the transition from improvisation towards composing something which has its own identity and can be sung again and again by the composer or by other people.

Another strategy is to record the child singing on tape. This is useful if the song is too hard to reproduce again, either because of its length, or use of indefinite pitches, or rhythmically unpredictable character. Listening to the song to see what it sounds like helps to introduce the idea of reviewing work, as one might a construction in Lego.

If a child finds it hard just to think of a song, the teacher can stage the process by helping the child make some simple words first and then, to use Davies' (ibid.)phrase to '*say it till a song comes*'. By saying the words rhythmically and experimenting with different ways of singing them, gradually a song will appear.

listen for

- how the child manages finding rhythms for the words:
  do the rhythm patterns match up with a natural word stress?
  what character or feel do they give the text?
- how the word strings fit into musical phrases:
  do some words extend the musical line further than sounds convincing, 'going off the end of the music'?

- the melodic shapes used:
  is the pitch aspect fully melodic or somewhere between speech, chant and song? if it's fully song, what kind of melodic shapes are used? do some melodic ideas recur? what is the range of notes used?
- what the structure of the whole song is like:
  is it rambling? are there phrases? what lengths are they? do they repeat? is there a verse structure?
- how the song ends, if it does....

In a later study (1992), Davies identifies some significant features found in songs invented by 5–7-year-olds:

- a sense of 'closure' with a range of techniques for bringing songs to an end – tailing off into words, using falling phrases, ending with several repeated notes;
- frequent use of 4-phrase structures – the structure found in many simple songs and nursery rhymes;
- patterns of repetition and alternation;
- transformations in the use of musical ideas.

| notice |

- what the song shows about the child's previous experience of songs;
- how the child sings; how the song is limited by *i)* language ability *ii)* vocal ability;
- the inventiveness shown with both words and music.

| intervention |

In order to move children's song composing forward, the teacher must focus children's attention on listening to their own songs and noticing what they've done, for example, as indicated in the 'listen to' section above. The teacher's role here is to reflect back to the child what the listener hears, to describe the musical features of the song, without value judgement. Making judgements about how 'good' it is belongs to much later stages. Listening together to the song on tape is very useful here.

To begin with, drawing attention to just one feature might be quite enough: *'you sang the bit that went "wagged her tail" twice'* or *'you ended on a really long note'*. This works towards the child gradually building the idea that you make a song just like you make a picture, choosing what goes where, and looking at it as a whole. With a song, the choices are made by listening and then deciding on the rhythm and speed, the melody shape and tone of voice, and the structure of repetitions, verses, choruses.

progression

Once the idea of song-making is established and children become used to making songs and noticing features of them, the teacher can help them build their understanding of different ways songs can be made. Comparisons can be made with songs in the class repertoire. Recorded songs can be listened to and discussed as compositions. Using the ideas resulting from these investigations, children can try making:

- call and response songs;
- two way conversation songs;
- single verse songs;
- songs in verses where the tune repeats but the words don't;
- songs with verses and chorus.

As with all composition teaching, there is a delicate balance between introducing ideas and techniques and allowing children to make their own decisions about the end result. The key to fostering compositional development is consistently to leave composers to make all decisions whilst increasing awareness of different possibilities and of the bases on which decisions can be taken. If teachers work with a standardised model of what they think 'sounds right', children end up composing only what fits the model and all imaginative qualities are lost. Children readily become their own judges once they begin to understand how the music works.

composing for voice sounds

Using the voice as an instrument capable of a huge range of different sounds opens up another set of composition opportunities, as in the Meredith Monk pieces below. Unlike other instruments, the voice has associations with the whole gamut of human expression, going far beyond expression with words. Young children are still particularly close to wordless vocal expression. They have no difficulty in enjoying making and listening to voice sounds, just for their own qualities.

Plenty of composers have used the range of vocal timbres in just this way. Children can improvise and compose using:
- humming;
- voice sliding;
- rhythmic breathing;
- tongue clicks;
- music using letter sounds:
  consonants made with lips, tongue, teeth, vowels made with mouth shape and voice.

Investigating another composer's music based on vocal timbre will help to extend children's ideas. The following approach can be used with any example from the nursery's or school's collection.

●————————————————————————————

Meredith Monk: Facing North

[CD ECM Records ECM 1482 437439-2]

How many different ways can we sing without words? How many different sounds can voices make?

Sometimes music is made by voices used just as instruments. It reminds us how expressive they can be without saying anything.

choice of music

This music uses a wide range of extended vocal techniques, in a very clear, accessible and evocative way. Meredith Monk is an American composer who works across a spectrum of music, performance art and music theatre. Facing North is a set of pieces, mainly for two voices. It was first performed in concert; later Monk devised visual and movement ideas which arose from the music and the piece was performed 'as chamber music/a music theatre piece about a barren wilderness and the fortitude and tenderness of two people surviving within it' (Monk, CD notes). It is interesting how the writing of this music illustrates the complexity of a process we often overuse with children, as if it were simple. Here Monk started from an experience of snow, and the silence and stillness which it brings. She developed the music from a range of sound qualities produced by the voice, a capella. She says 'As I worked, I tried to evoke the elemental, bracing clarity of the northern landscape. I realised then that "north" is also a state of mind'.

<table>
<tr><td>

starting points

</td><td>

Before hearing the music, do some introductory work on making and controlling different voice sounds. This might start with humming and finding at least six different shades of humming sounds, hearing them from the inside and listening to other people making them. Next try a whole range of other voice sounds, experimenting with using more or less breath in the sound, with mouths open or closed, and with making the sound from the chest and from the head, higher and lower and so on. Include whispers, short syllables used rhythmically, consonant and vowel sounds.

[Facing North is a collection of ten short pieces. They could be listened to like a story, one a day, wondering what comes next. The shortest is 32 seconds, the longest 5 and a half minutes. Each uses voice sounds in different and imaginative ways. Arctic Bar starts with a simple umpah piano, joined in turn by a very high voice, vocal rhythmic effects and organ. Later we hear a panting sound – a husky dog, rhythmically out of breath? Monk's music is based on a minimalist approach of developing the music from repetition of short motifs and playing with simple pattern ideas, differently combined and layered.]

</td></tr>
</table>

investigate

- how this composer uses the voice: the sounds made and how they're made; *try 'sound spotting' and collect as many as you can; try performing them yourselves;*
- the expressive effects of these sounds; *what do they conjure up? for each of us different things perhaps?*
- the idea of starting with very simple patterns; *how does the music go on with these? what happens?*
- the idea of a set of small pieces: *how do they connect with each other?*

go on to

- make some movement or images to go with the music.

learning to sing songs

Song singing is the backbone of musical experience in the early years of schooling for most young children. Singing is not only valuable in itself but the songs themselves also provide a means for learning about music. It is no surprise that many music education approaches promote song singing as the best start to music education. Singing vibrates within, it leaves sensations and memory traces which can support musical understanding at all stages.

Newly arrived at the start of the year, nursery and reception children may find whole class and whole school singing sessions quite bewildering. For learning to sing, like every other curriculum area, the child needs first footholds and graded introductory steps. Early years teachers understand well the need for carefully measured out introductions in areas such as reading and number work and this pedagogical understanding should also be applied to singing.

For young children, learning to sing a song involves a network of skills and knowledges. It is worth looking at these in detail:

- aural – to listen attentively to learn the song and to self-monitor singing;
- physical – to control breathing and the vocal mechanism;
- verbal – to remember, understand, pronounce the song words;
- musical memory – to remember musical forms and reproduce them;
- performing – to produce rhythm, pitch patterns, dynamics and tonal qualities with sensitivity and accuracy;
- social – to cooperate in singing activities with others;
- communicative – to sing expressively with and to others.

Considering these many demands one begins to understand how complex a learning process the singing of a song can be. Studies of this process have shown that a child's interest is at first focused upon the text of the song (Welch, 1997). Everyday knowledge of working with children tells teachers that children first struggle to get hold of the words. Next the child appears to capture the rhythmic detail of the song and only finally to concentrate on the melodic detail. Knowing that the melody is last in line for attention will shape teachers' choice of approaches for song learning and the choice of songs. Song words should be quick to learn and easily pronounced and might be put on one side while melody only is listened to and learnt. Such teaching approaches will be looked at later.

In addition to the learning sequence of 'words, rhythm, then melody' common to most, individual children will have different learning styles. So, one child who has not yet discovered how to produce a singing sound may have verbal facility and quickly learns the words. Another may respond to the rhythmic vitality of the song with body movement. Some may listen attentively and rarely sing but reproduce the song on other occasions (at home, in the playground) while others even at an early age will manage the whole song with relative ease. This is the usual spectrum of participation from young children. Differentiating across such a band of abilities sets challenges for the teacher. En masse singing is unlikely to create opportunities for catering for each child as an individual singer at their own stage of development and with their own way of approaching song learning.

Most research into children's singing development has focused upon the ability to learn to sing in tune, for this has been a dominant area of interest for some time. Yet this is just one voice-music skill out of many. Until recently much discussion of out-of-tune singing was couched in negative terms as if this was some kind of incurable deficiency. Now, with better understanding of children's singing abilities, children are termed 'developing singers' (Welch, 1997) who can be placed somewhere along a continuum of ever-increasing vocal competence. Having difficulties in finding the singing voice and learning to pitch with accuracy represent the earlier stages where some children might be 'stuck' and in need of extra help rather than already labelled as non-singers, a fact of nature.

children as developing singers

While holding in mind that children's singing development fans out across a web of different skills and knowledges, two specific pathways of their developing singing are useful to know. The first is the development of the pitch range of young children's singing voices. This will guide teachers' choice of voice activities and song repertoire and is also helpful for assessing children.

In broad stages the child can:
- find the singing voice;
- sing on just one or two pitches (chanting);
- sing in a small range of notes, usually at a fairly low pitch (around D above middle C);
- sing in a wider range of notes, middle C or D to five notes higher, G or A;
- sing an extended range of pitches, lifting the voice higher over a register break to B flat and above (Moore, 1994).

Of course children can swoop and shriek their voices to reach a very wide pitch range but can usually best control their vocal pitch in the voice ranges described here.

Notice that the pitch range at which children are most likely to sing successfully is both narrow and quite low. Many of the songs traditionally sung in early years settings cover too wide a pitch range (Victor Smith, 1996) for children with developing voices to manage. These early years songs may well be sung to and with children for other purposes, as a story song, for movement or for a game, but if the teaching intention is for children to sing with pitch accuracy, songs should be carefully chosen to fall within the child's current vocal range. Careful listening and constant adjusting of the song, a little higher, a little lower will enable teachers to match song to children.

Learning to sing songs not only asks the child to find a singing voice of many notes but to also be able to hear an outside pitch and control the voice to match the same sound (vocal pitch-matching). Many 4 and 5-year-olds for example, can reproduce melodies at their own pitch and sing them solo with accuracy but cannot always sing in tune with a given pitch. That skill develops along another pathway. In the singing of relatively simple children's songs, the words are at first the prime focus of the child's interest, then the child begins to be able to follow roughly the shape of the song melody listened to. Later the child may be able to reproduce the song melody with accuracy but sings it at a pitch too low or too high. Finally the child can pitch-match the voice with accuracy.

If children are to learn to control and pitch-match their voices they must be able to listen to and monitor their own singing. Singing alone, with a partner or small group enables children to hear their own voices. Without accompaniment is best. The heavy sound of a piano overwhelms young voices so that careful listening to self is barely possible. A guitar is lighter and the player can face the children. Possible too is a touch of folk melodeon or Indian harmonium.

tailoring teaching to support the developing singer

Given the recent and growing awareness of children as developing singers, careful thought should be given to teaching approaches for learning to sing songs. One of the most important aspects of working with children as singers is to make the learning process explicit, not only to suggest tasks but to involve children in the purpose of each activity. Making it clear to children why something is being practised or tried out is important. Handing back the initiative to children wherever possible gives them the opportunity to suggest ways to practise. They can listen to alternatives, make choices and decide how a song should be performed. All too often these decisions are handled only by the teacher and valuable opportunities are lost to develop children's independent understanding and awareness of song singing.

In developing approaches to song learning the teacher can aim to:
- create an environment for singing;
  The classroom needs to be a place where everyone sings comfortably and freely. Attitudes towards singing should be positive and relaxed.

- provide frequent opportunities for practice;
  Little and often as part of the everyday classroom timetable is better than single long sessions.

- listen carefully to each child and consider each child as an individual song-singer.
  Adjust teaching input to each individual child.

- match the child's singing and extend it;
  The child's current vocal capability is the starting point e.g. the teacher sings the same note, or melodic fragment as the child and draws attention to the matching of the two voices; then extends the task by asking the child to sing just the next-door note or perhaps a slightly changed fragment.

- focus on the direction of pitch movement;
  Children first grasp a sense of pitch direction before matching single pitches. Introduce activities in which the voice slides up or down or in rising and falling shapes. Following the pitch direction with hand movement adds visual emphasis.

- echo sing short melodic units;
  Children will remember short chunks of melody more easily and accurately than whole song melodies. The units can be taken from songs they are about to learn and then slotted back into the whole.

- practise the melody line without the words;
  To enable the children to focus attention upon the melody, sing it without the words, to vocables.

- provide verbal feedback;
  Encouragement and an atmosphere of positive achievement is important. Children should also receive specific feedback which refers to pitch matching, tone quality, voice technique etc. upon which they can build an awareness of their own singing abilities.

- encourage children to self-monitor their own singing;
  Encourage perceptive listening to their own singing and to the singing of others. Help them to comment on aspects of their own or others' singing.

- provide visual imagery.
  Gestures, handsigns, drawn shapes and notations will support the child's emerging awareness of pitch directions.

Planning for variable practice, in which the song is approached from many different directions is the basis for successful learning on the part of children. Song learning sessions can be planned to include solo and group singing opportunities, listening and commenting times, separation of the song into different parts and layers for specific focus and then singing for a game or movement. And the pleasure of singing for its own sake should not be forgotten. Learning new songs and working at singing skills should be balanced by singing again those which are well known, for the pleasure and satisfaction that brings.

singing with a partner

Paired work for song singing presents the child with a new set of valuable challenges which are not possible when the whole class sings as one. Most of the decisions which are usually handled by the teacher are now handed back to the child:

- what note to begin on?
- at what speed, loudness, to sing?
- with what vocal timbre to sing?
- how to practise?
- how to begin together, keep together and end together?
- what kind of accompaniment is needed?

– and other aspects of performance. Paired work also frees up the teacher to attend as listener and to monitor each child's individual progress as a singer. Tucked away as one of a large group those who need specific support in the process of learning to sing are not always spotted.

The following song makes an excellent song for singing with a partner, suitable for those who are still fairly limited in vocal range. It can be introduced as a story song and works well in this way with the youngest song listeners.

partner song: dumplins

A traditional song in Jamaican nation language (Christian and Burnett, 1981).

one of me Dump-lin's gone. Don't tell me so. One of me Dump-lin's gone. Don't tell me so. One of me Dump-lin's gone!

starting points

Gather the children around with the same sense of coming together and readiness as at story times. Knowing the song well, taking time to present the song in such a way that it comes alive is important. The song can be sung with free, speech-like rhythms in a dramatic style. Taking time to look at each child during the song singing conveys a sense of singing for each one as an individual.

Each child pretends to have made four dumplins. At every repetition of the verse another dumplin disappears; an opportunity for some number thinking. The children soon recognise the cumulative story the song is telling and begin to anticipate the next disappearance. It doesn't take long for one or two to puzzle out who the thief must be.

Most young children will gradually join in of their own accord, usually contributing the fragments of song which they pick up most readily. The short phrase, 'don't tell me so' is the most accessible snatch to sing first. They will gradually absorb the song from repeat hearings. Older children can learn the song by echoing it section by section.

The words, 'Cookie you see nobody pass here' are cumbersome but retain the original language. If the song is sung slowly with flexible rhythm the words are soon manageable.

with a partner

The song is a call and response dialogue between two characters, the child and the 'cookie'. Children can be encouraged to communicate the mini-drama of the song by the way they perform it, the tone quality of their voices, the dynamics they choose – and show their growing frustration at the disappearing dumplins and the nonchalance of the guilty 'cookie'.

| listen for |

Each child's ability to:
- remember and reproduce the melody line, how accurately?
- match their voice pitching to their partner;
- begin their part at the right moment and sing at the same tempo;
- sing with variety of tone colour and dynamic in order to convey the expressive character of the song;
- stand with good posture, breathe well;

| intervention |

Visiting the paired singers and listening carefully against the 'listen for' points given above will tell the teacher what support and appropriate input is needed by each child. For example, that for the second singer, the word 'no' can be difficult to pitch and here the teacher may wish to quietly prompt the singing. Included as one of a rotation sequence of activities over a few weeks partner singing can provide an opportunity for the teacher to make brief notes on each child as a singer.

learning voice skills

The activities in this section are for warming the voice and extending voice techniques. They not only loosen and ready the body and vocal mechanism for all kinds of voice music but also create an atmosphere of calm with alertness for what follows. Most are intended as starters, not as free-standing activities.

Making voice technique explicit to children during the activities is important; using the voice depends upon hidden and quite mysterious processes. Yet even the youngest child can work, for example, at sitting well, without hunched shoulders and at breathing games which draw on the familiar such as blowing candles out.

activities

body-ready?

- relax the shoulders and gently loosen the neck by tipping the head slowly and carefully from side to side;
  drop the arms by the side and shake loosely;

- stand upright, feet slightly apart OR sit with an upright but not stiff posture (to stand for voice work is best, small chairs are preferable, cross-legged on the floor usually results in a hunched position);

- relax the lower jaw by yawning, soften the lips and tongue with repetitive syllables: mm, mm, mmm,
                                        ma, ma, ma;
  try out different consonants, how do the mouth parts work to produce them?

breathing-ready?

- relax the throat, breathe in, make soft husky growls, emphasise the effect with loose, open body movements (which help to avoid the tense humping of shoulders which often accompanies breathing in);

- practise breathing from the diaphragm with some long slow breaths, slowly exhale avoiding any tension; (lying on the floor can help to focus attention on the feel of breathing from the stomach);
  letting the air out with a hisssss – is fun;
  holding a finger up to the mouth to feel the stream of air encourages control;

- practise breath control by singing soft vowel sounds on a long breath of air, loooo, taaaa (at any pitch);
now start quietly and get louder, squeeze out the sound but don't force it;

- pant like a dog, then try to attach a singing sound (Victor-Smith, 1996);

- sing this song; at the end breathe in slowly and 'puff' out the fire.

voice-ready?

- start with a high note and slide the pitch down in a glide (Durrant and Welch, 1995); use a hand gesture to emphasise the pitch direction;

- hum, just feel the buzzing sensation in the throat, hum a very low note and feel the sensation, then rise up slowly;
'Land' a hum from high to low, hum vocal shapes which rise and fall;

- sing this song and play with the shape of the 'mmm' at the end.

In the sections which follow, each of the examples introduce activities which extend children's understanding of different vocal possibilities.

focus on voice skills: The Swan

As children's voice skills develop they will be ready to tackle more challenging songs. This miniature song of simple, melodic elegance is suitable for more experienced singers whose vocal range spans the octave and who have worked on breathing control.

The swan sings tir-e-li—o   tir-e-li—o   tir-e-li—o

starting points

Before singing, prepare with some of the breathing activities given in the list above. The song should ideally be carried through on one breath with a very smooth, sustained tone. Good voice control will also help the children to manage the leap from lowest to highest note at the beginning without forcing the tone on the top note.

the singing

- Listen to the song. Close your eyes and just listen. Listen carefully again.
- Watch the shape of the melody as you listen once more. Use smooth flowing gestures to shape the melodic line.
- Hear the three notes which sit on the same pitch at the beginning. Listen to the melody reaching up to the highest note and then slipping down note by note in a sequence. Children could look at a notated version of the song at this point.
- Body and voice ready? Stand well and breathe well. Carry the song through on one breath if possible. Try. Practise. Listen to half the group singing. Talk about the singing sound. What tempo seems right for the song? and for voice control?
- Sing with various vocables
  e.g. the swan sings noo, noo noo noo
  naa naa etc.
  and listen to voice tone.
- In small groups, listen to others sing the song and give constructive feedback.

go on to

Sing the first motif repeatedly as a melodic ostinato. Others sing the whole song.

Singing a vocal ostinato in this way is a good first step into part singing. Later children can take another small chunk of the song, one of the 'tirelio' motifs and sing that over and over as an ostinato. Hearing the timbres and the textures as the voices in a capella group weave together begins to build up children's sense of how part-singing sounds. Even while they are still in only the very early stages of singing in parts themselves, children can enjoy listening to harmonic singing, perhaps particularly with unaccompanied voices.

focus on part-singing: Paul Simon and Ladysmith Black Mombasa – Homeless

[from the album Gracelands: Warner Bros. 925447-2]

As an example, the skill of the vocal group, Ladysmith Black Mombasa, makes the melodic and rhythmic layering and overlapping of this music sound almost easy to do. The richness and depth of the voices and the range of vocal effects which are drawn into the singing give enormous scope for enjoying, joining in, and for discussion about how the sounds are made. There are examples of call and response singing and use of repeating structures with repetitions which are differently coloured with vocal effects. The contrast of vocal styles between Paul Simon and Ladysmith Black Mombasa adds another dimension and raises issues about fusions of musical styles from different cultures.

starting points

Find and sing a call and response song (see example on p. 144). Let the children become really familiar with the song and if there are willing volunteers, encourage children to take the leading role, singing the call part solo with the rest of the class answering. Tape record the singing and let the children listen and discuss the effect of hearing one voice answered by many voices. Go on to discuss how this song structure is often associated with work songs with the music helping the workers to keep going and to coordinate the work actions rhythmically.

[The song Homeless begins with an introduction of a solo voice, answered by a chorus, with extra voice effects. A spoken 'Sing!' leads into the next section which is built on a verse which has two short, two-note phrases 'homeless, homeless', answered by a longer one. The verse repeats and the solo voice fills in between each phrase, giving a different kind of solo verse dialogue. The last section has a solo 'somebody sing' call answered by the chorus and coloured by yet more vocal effects. All the melodic shapes are falling ones, giving a relaxed feel to the whole piece, despite its serious text. A description such as this doesn't convey anything of the vocal timbres and effects: the music must be listened to and allowed to speak for itself.]

| investigate | • how the use of solo voice and chorus is different in each section: *try out some of these ideas using songs you know;* |

- how all the different voice sounds are made and controlled: *try making them for yourself;*
- the idea of using layers of voices in part singing: *the voices, all male, range from very low to very high; can you hear the different parts singing different tunes? do they move together or at different times, with different rhythms?*
- how the words seem to fit naturally with the rhythm and the melody;
- the idea of making melodies from two short phrases balanced by one longer one: *try making your own melodies like this, using voices or instruments.*

| go on to | • listen to more music for chorus or part singing. |

● ──

example of a call and response song: Sansa Kroma

In a call and response song two singers, or a lead singer and a group, take turns. Here, in this song, the call: 'Sansa Kroma' is followed by the response: 'Ne na wu‿o...'. The call always remains the same and its five note range makes it suitable for developing singers who have not yet found their wider singing range. Other singers with more vocal versatility could take the response. Older children might partner younger singers for paired singing (like paired reading).

This song originates from the Akan people of Ghana and was transcribed into notation by Abraham Kobena Adzenyah (1997).

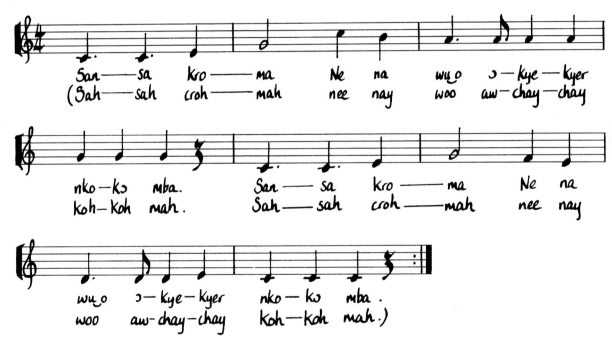

Like many Ghanaian children's songs this one carries teaching about the values of Akan society. The song tells of the young hawks children see flying overhead in search of chicks to kill, having to fend for themselves. And it reminds the children that if anything happened to their parents they would not have to roam alone looking after themselves, a relative in their own village would take them in.

Listen to a recording which offers good models of the performance style for this song or other Ghanaian songs. Adzinyah with others have recorded the songs. This singing group is not expecting to produce a homogeneous choir sound, each individual singer will sound as themselves and have their own individual timbre.

The song is part of an oral/aural tradition of song-singing and as such would not be fixed in one written version as given here. In practice, performances of this song are likely to be many-varied, different on each occasion according to the time, place, people and mood. The questions can be asked, '*how shall we sing the song today?*' '*who do we have here, how do we feel?*'

Any transcription fixes the rhythms and pitches rigidly. Once known, practise singing the song with a flexible, fluid rhythmic style. Improvising gentle side to side movements while singing will help to give the song a rhythmic 'feel'.

the game

A stone passing game can be played with the song. Sitting in a circle each child has a pebble which they tap on the floor twice in front and then pass to the right.

Tap Tap Pass (Rest)

When children can do this pattern they might be able to put a clap in the rest. A gankogui (bell) can tap out the same rhythm of tap, tap, pass (rest).

The final three short sections consider aspects of planning and providing for song singing. They look specifically at questions which may need to be asked to ensure the child's involvement in song-singing, at factors which will guide the choice of repertoire and at setting up an area for making music with the voice.

the child's involvement in song-singing

If children are genuinely to sing as independent, competent and confident singers then their involvement in the range of song-singing opportunities should be carefully considered. The following list of questions aims to highlight some of the areas which may need to be thought about:

- has the child chosen the song, helped to choose it?
- does the child find the song enjoyable and meaningful?
- has the child had enough time to listen, learn and practise singing the song?
- is the child able to contribute to interpretation and performance decisions, such as: the tempo, pitch range, timbral quality, changes in dynamics and other expressive characteristics?
- can the child sing songs with their own stamp of individuality? in their own performance style?
- does the child have the chance to sing songs in their own language, dialect and from their own culture? to find themselves in songs in a range of non-stereotypical roles of gender, race and physical ability?
- are there opportunities given to the child to sing songs for many different purposes which have significance for the child – birthdays, special days, for new shoes, for sadness at a pet's death?
- does the child have the opportunity not to sing the song sometimes, but to choose to listen again to others singing it or to a recording?

choosing repertoire

When a staff member gathers to choose voice repertoire for each year group there are several factors which will affect choice:

- the children's singing abilities;
  is the song in a suitable pitch range?
  is the level of difficulty appropriate?
- ensuring a range of musical forms;
  story songs, call and response, lullabies, game songs, one-liners, first part-songs etc.;
- variety of musical elements;
  songs in different tempi, different metres, varying melodic shapes etc.;
- representing a range of times and places;
- gender, race and physical ability;
  songs words which avoid stereotypical roles of gender, race and physical ability;
  signed words for hearing impaired children;

- language, dialect.
  songs as another way of bringing a rich variety of languages into classroom use, affirming cultural diversity.

---

providing for voice music

The idea of an area set up specially for music is well established in early years practice but such an area is usually equipped for music activity with instruments only. A singing area (perhaps with cushions, sag-bags, inside a booth or tent) is intended to encourage individual singing play. It might be equipped with:

- song and rhyme books: *traditional songs, game songs, silly songs, songs from other cultures and dual language song books*;
- singsong books (Andress, 1980): *books with pictures which will stimulate spontaneous song play*;
- singing dolls (Andress, 1980): *plain, simple wooden dolls but with open mouths as if singing*;
- singing puppets: *of various kinds which can mouth, oven mits or 'muppet-type' puppets work well* (Suthers, 1996);
- song cards: *cards with pictures which connect with songs the children know, for readers include suggestions for singing activities*;
- microphone: *a pretend one or real*;
- cassette player/listening centre: *for children to record their own singing or to listen to recordings*;
- blank tapes (short 3–5 minute type);
- cassettes/CDs: *of children's singing of known songs, of composed songs, voice pieces, or songs sung by others*;
- notations of known songs;
- pictures of male and female song-singers: *from song books, cassette/CD sleeves*;
- video recordings of people singing: *children singing, singing as part of worship, folk, pop, opera, country, jazz singers etc.*

assessment points

early stages

The child:
- can find a singing voice and vary the pitch of the singing voice to follow the melody line of known songs;
- can improvise spontaneous conversations with a partner;
- can control the voice in simple voice techniques (some control of breathing, producing a range of different voice sounds, standing well);
- can sing a number of one-liner and other short songs independently.

later stages

The child:
- can sing short songs with accuracy of pitch and rhythm and in tune with a given pitch;
- can make-up improvised songs;
- can control the voice in first voice techniques (how to breathe, stand well, singing tone);
- knows and can sing independently a range of songs, some from different places and times.

music with
instruments

Making music with instruments takes the child into a whole new sphere of musical possibilities. It is all too easy to view classroom instruments as just a collection of rather noisy hardware and to forget that each has its own musical potential and its own roots in the music of particular times and places.

Instrumental music takes us beyond the immediacy of musical experience with voice or movement. Instruments are used to produce sound as extensions of body action – striking, shaking, blowing – and have to be controlled through an entirely different set of skills, often requiring fine motor control. Even as infants children show a delight in making 'sound marks' on the world in these ways. The baby's play with a rattle, the discovery of the sounds made by banging with flat hands on a table surface, or, later, hitting two bricks together, demonstrate the roots of the enjoyment of instrumental sound. During the early years, this is built on as children learn to control the sounds made and use them in a musical context.

Children's interest in making music with instruments is often intense. The quite extraordinary range of timbres which instruments offer and the different musical capabilities of each kind of instrument are a challenge to both teacher and children if they are taken seriously. As with all work in music, the focus is on listening and the teacher needs constantly to reinforce this. What matters is that children learn to use instrumental sound musically; the instrument is just, as the word implies, a means to an end, though often a very beautiful and intriguing one.

Instrumental activity with young children will include:
- free play;
- improvising and composing;
- sorting instruments and sounds;
- accompanying singing with instruments;
- playing instruments with others;
- learning instrumental skills.

choosing instruments

Before looking at the different kinds of instrumental activity through which learning takes place, some thought needs to be given to the choice of instruments for classroom use. Instruments suggested for nursery use are often little more than toys. They should be 'real' instruments and of the best quality that can be managed. A mistaken idea is that they need to be small to handle; this doesn't follow. In some cases, larger instruments are easier to play than smaller ones. A range of size is essential in order to produce a range of sound. Although subsidiary to the sound considerations, the aesthetic appeal of an instrument in itself is important if children are to be encouraged to enjoy using it.

Choosing instruments involves:
- listening for a pleasing sound;
- considering the musical possibilities the instruments offer;
- looking, feeling the qualities of an instrument: is it good to look at, feel, handle? considering the examples of technology: carving, lacing, weaving of raffia, stringing, threading and sewing, metalwork and woodwork, plastics, and IT;
- ensuring instruments represent a range of times, places and cultural backgrounds;
- considering how they will be maintained and cared for, how durable and safe they are for use by early years children.

Listen carefully to the sound of the instrument. Play it, hold it. Does it make a sound which is pleasing, exciting, soothing, intriguing perhaps? Will it catch and hold the children's listening attention? Our own sensitivities to sound can become dulled; the quality of listening is vital in deciding what to choose and buy, what to keep or discard.

Instruments have different roles. For example, a pair of maracas, hand-held and shaken, is characteristically an instrument played by members of a group. It is a 'joining in with others' instrument where its sharp, crisp sound adds edge and timbre to the whole ensemble. For a child playing alone it may be less successful. The bongos (double-headed drums), on the other hand, work well as a solo instrument. They can be played with a variety of hand strikes and arm movements. Action patterns of left or right hand alternately or hands together can be explored.

Some infant schools have a legacy of 'band trolley' instruments, a number of miniaturised versions of military band or orchestral percussion instruments. The sound from these instruments is usually poor and there is little to be gained from the 'one each' and all playing together approach of the percussion band. Don't be afraid to throw away poor quality instruments.

Choice of instruments should offer a balanced range of playing actions: not just striking, but plucking, shaking, scraping and, with care for hygiene, blowing. Each way of playing gives a characteristic set of sounds; leaving one group out is like leaving colours out of the paintbox.

Some instruments, particularly those which are hand-made and imported from overseas, are wonderful artefacts in themselves. Who made them? Who carved for so long to hollow out this drum, or made the leather thongs which bind the skin to tightly to its frame? Hand-made objects carry with them a sense of the maker and the place of making.

Equally there are exciting technologies to explore. How do drum mats respond so instantly to the first touch of a toe or the sound beam whisked into sound by a finger moving across the invisible beam? Synthesised sound and the playing possibilities available on computers with soundcards introduce another dimension again, though the connection with body action is much less direct. Larger drum machines with pads are a better form of access to music technology for younger children.

Instruments can be adapted for children with all kinds of disabilities. Different ways of supporting instruments on stands or body and different ways of enabling children to use beaters can be devised. Music technology offers enormous scope for disabled children (Ellis, 1987, 1995). Large play structures allow children to use whole body movements to produce sound (Dale, 1995).

free play

The opportunity to play freely with instruments is absolutely essential if children are to develop skills and understanding in using them. There is no substitute for having quiet, uninterrupted time in which to explore and absorb a detailed knowledge of the instrument's potential and how it feels to play it. Even as adults we know this for ourselves. Introduced to a new instrument, the first impulse is to try it out, at first just playing with it, being curious, delighting in discoveries, and enjoying 'messing about'.

> Ellen, four years, played for almost twenty minutes on a xylophone set in the middle of a group of tables set out for dough play, pencils and paper for writing and potato printing. First she swung the beater high and slammed it slowly onto the keys. Very fast regular two handed playing followed. Noticing that one key bounced in its fixing, she struck deliberately on the edge of the key to make other keys bounce. After this she struck the end wood of the instrument, surprised by its hollow sound and played all around the wooden sides. She removed all the keys, one by one and replaced them. Suddenly she stood up to play, swinging the beaters wide and singing 'da da da' as she played.

These initial stages quickly lead on to the desire to control the sound better and to find ways of producing just the desired effect. Acquiring some skill becomes strategic in avoiding frustration. As techniques are learnt, again a free rein is needed to allow practice at the individual's own speed and in their own way.

Such opportunities are not so hard to provide for if the approach is thought through. A jumble of instruments with too many children elbowing each other out of the way to get a turn, making a lot of clatter in an already noisy classroom, leads nowhere. Two priorities in providing for free musical play are:
- children need to work alone, or in a pair at most if they are collaborating;
- the quietest available space is best.

Planning for quiet instead of for noise is important if children are to be able to listen to themselves. By and large they play in quieter, more controlled ways if they can hear what they're doing. Next is to realise that the instrument itself will play a key part in structuring the child's activity. Much of children's classroom play is centred on using apparatus which in itself focuses their learning, for example in maths; in just the same way, each musical instrument will offer a particular musical focus. For example, a tuned, barred instrument such as a xylophone gives a visual analogue of notes arranged in pitch order and can be rigged to offer a chosen musical scale – major, minor, pentatonic or modal.

Teachers can provide for children's learning by:
- offering single instruments, selected according to their musical potential;
- offering small sets of instruments which focus one musical aspect;
- allowing for many re-visits so that children become familiar with the instruments;
- rotating available instruments over time, changing perhaps every fortnight, or less often if interest is maintained; making instruments available if asked for when not on offer;
- encouraging children to listen hard as they play;
- allowing opportunities for feedback and discussion about the sounds and music made with particular instruments.

As children play with an instrument, they gradually build up their ideas of cause and effect: *'If I do this, then I hear that'*. In the early stages, they just 'do' the music, thinking of it in action as it's played. Teachers can encourage children to listen and focus on the sound that results from these actions, talking about it in musical terms: *'The tune went higher and higher…'* . By listening to the sound as feedback, children can experiment and refine their actions to produce the sounds and patternings they want.

There is also a role for teachers as 'play partners', listening to or joining in with children's activity, but supporting rather than leading it. Just listening attentively, when it comes at the right moment, is in itself a powerful way of giving encouragement. Or a game of taking turns might emerge, in which the teacher picks up on the child's musical ideas, as a 'copycat', or 'going on from', or slightly changing or developing them. This is a way of wordlessly reinforcing what the child is doing, highlighting how the music has been heard by someone else and helping to model techniques of playing the instrument. A *'will you please play me...'* format is a slightly stronger form of intervention which can be used to revisit and focus on musical ideas the child has been using; e.g. *'will you please play me a mixture of those jingly sounds and the little taps I heard just now?'*.

Every instrument is different. Avoid from the start any idea that one instrument will do instead of another or that 'we'll use some instruments' as if it doesn't matter which ones we choose. Young children are highly sensitive to differences in timbre and unless they have some hearing impairment are able to discriminate between sounds much more finely than adults. So instruments can be introduced as individuals, each with their own enormous repertoire of sound possibilities. Far from asking children to tell a high sound from a low, or a loud from a quiet, or, worst of all, a xylophone from a triangle, the expectation must be that they practise discriminating finely across the whole range of what each individual instrument can do. In this respect, the attitude of composers and performers should be adopted: that it always matters precisely which sounds are chosen and how they are made and controlled.

Free play with instruments contributes to learning in the early stages of:
● understanding sounds and how they are made;
● becoming familiar with the range of timbre, pitch, duration, and dynamics which each different instrument can produce;
● selecting and using sounds to invent music;
● controlling sounds in order to perform music.

some examples of instruments and settings:

~ a baritone xylophone (larger size) with several soft beaters positioned in the middle of a number of tables set out for a range of activities;
exploring melodic scales and shapes, playing patterns, using larger-scale playing actions;

~ a basket of gourd and seed-pod instruments to shake and rattle in different ways;
exploring different timbres and pitches of rattles, shaking techniques;

- a pair of bongos positioned on a small table at one side;
  finding pitch and rhythm patterns made with one and two handed playing actions; using different finger actions to produce the sound;

- chimes, bells and metal gongs, slung from a climbing frame or similar wooden frame to be played upright with small beaters;
  discovering variations in timbre, pitch and dynamics among metal sounds; enjoying their resonance; learning how to stop the sounds to alter their duration; making music from long sounds;

- a set of drums of different heights set out in a semicircular array like a kit, standing in a large play space outdoors for active play;
  discovering patterns made from combinations of drum sounds; exploring different hand and arm actions for making sounds;

- steel-pan slung at low height with sticks for playing;
  finding the different pitches which each section produces; making melodic patterns from an instrument which presents notes in a different order (not as a scale);

- guitar laid flat on the floor so that children can feel the vibrations of the sound box as it is played (children with impaired hearing can lay close to it to hear sounds and feel vibrations);
  making rhythm patterns of plucking and strumming actions; making melodic patterns and harmonic textures; starting and stopping the sound;

- a sound mat set out as part of bouncy cushions for bare feet play;
  dancing on the mats to create stepping patterns of differently pitched sounds;

- instruments to wear and dance with – ghungroo, morris bells, seed pod waistlet, anklets and bracelets;
  making bell and rattle music from movement patterns;

- sound beam equipment in free movement area;
  creating and controlling electronic sounds by moving in the beam; imaginative possibilities for children with impaired movement;

~ outdoor music play structures – permanent and weather proof; *using large body movements to produce percussive sound; making slow music.*

Provision might also include loan instruments to be used for music and studied as artefacts as well.

improvising and composing with individual instruments

As soon as a child becomes familiar with using an instrument, the more random kinds of free play become interspersed with patterning and repetitions of short musical ideas. The nature of these ideas is influenced both by the structure of the instrument itself and by the kind of action patterns the child uses to play it. These improvisations are a form of music making in their own right and form the basis for composing at a later stage.

Mai Yi, five years, spent a long time just playing with the xylophone. Gradually a pattern of using four adjacent notes emerged, moving down by step from high to low. She tried this starting at a number of different places on the instrument. If she started too low it went off the end. She clearly decided that it was best played beginning on the very top note of all and did it twice over. This gave her the idea of doing the opposite; starting with the lowest note on the instrument, she played a row of four notes which moved up, also twice over. At this point it seemed as if she became aware of the whole length of the xylophone and saw that there were some notes in the middle which hadn't yet been touched. She played the descending version of her four note pattern on these. As if to say 'and that's enough of all that' she finished her playing with a glissando effect, sliding her beater quickly to and fro across the whole instrument, a kind of scribble effect. The sound of this made her and some nearby children, who were by this time listening, giggle with pleasure.

In this case, as so often, finding a pattern or idea leads on to inventing a stream of music based on it, or even a whole piece which is complete in itself. The music may emerge from:

a visual pattern e.g. tapping all the way round the head of a drum,
an action pattern e.g. alternating a pluck and a strum,
a number pattern e.g. 'I do three of this and four of that'.

(Glover, 1993)

} Michael, four years, was playing a pair of Indian bells tied together with a string and held in his fist. He shook his hand in a clear and definite rhythm pattern of longer and shorter beats, which was repeated over and over again. What the listeners heard was a lot of jangling; the pattern itself was visible but barely audible.

At this stage, the teacher's role as a listener, who can reflect back to children how they've heard the music, is crucial in moving children forward. Whether the child's music is an ongoing stream of ideas or a more clear cut piece, the teacher can:

- pick out a musical idea and sing or play it back e.g. *'do you remember the bit that goes...?'*
  This allows the child to listen to it and 'recognise' the sound.
- pick out a musical aspect and describe it, introducing vocabulary, or ask the child to describe it.
  This helps the child to begin to conceptualise how music is structured.
- notice, but not comment on, some musical features which indicate emergent use of a melodic, rhythmic etc. idea.
  Use this as a cue to introduce and discuss the idea with the class later. This enables the teacher to match small inputs to an indication of what the child is ready for.

It is particularly important in the case of instrumental music that children are encouraged not only to listen as they work, but also to remember and internalise sounds in their 'mind's ear'. Musical imagination draws on the ability to hear sound in our head and this in turn rests on a rich store of deeply impressed sound experiences. Look for appropriate moments to ask children to *'listen to this and then think it in your head'* or *'play that bit, hear it in your head, and then play it again'*. Ask children if they remember the sound of the tambourine when they were using it? ' *What was it like? Can you think of the sound still now?'* Follow this by hearing the real thing. *'Is it how you thought it was?'*

<table>
<tr><td>

listen for

</td><td>

- use of a range of timbres;
- musical patterning and the sound result of other kinds of patterning;
- repetitions of ideas which return;
- parts of the musical stream which sound more ordered than the rest.

</td></tr>
<tr><td>

notice

</td><td>

- how much control of the instrument there is;
- where the child's attention is; is it listening attention?

</td></tr>
</table>

later stages

Hand in hand with improvisation and the emergence of compositional ideas comes the development of instrumental technique. These are interdependent. The increasing ability to manage the instrument and to control the sound opens up a wider range of musical possibilities e.g. a glockenspiel melody which jumps, played at a fast tempo; controlling dynamics enough to make an echo piece. Growing interest and confidence in creating music leads to the need to acquire and practise techniques for playing. By this time, children are ready to 'choose an instrument to make up some music', a stage on from free play in that the intention is focused towards improvising or composing.

Two opposite strategies can be useful here:
- improvising first to see what ideas come, then building the music from these;
  This is the way Mai Yi (above) worked. The melody patterns in her music were found while she was just playing with the instrument. She then turned her findings into a composition. Sanjit's music (below) remained an improvisation.

 Sanjit(5) had set out two small drums and a tambourine around him on the floor. At first he just went round and round these in order, tapping them with a beater. As he played rhythmic patterns started to come, mixtures of whole and half beats (always both on the same drum). The quite different sound of the tambourine led to it taking on a different role in the music as a way of punctuating the other rhythm patterns at the end of a phrase or as an 'accent ' in the middle. The music went on being improvised, but using a consistent repertoire of punctuated rhythm patterns.

- planning the music first, then trying out the plan.
  This encourages children to try to hear the music in their head before they make it. Later this is important for the compositional skill of managing the overall structure of a piece. An example of a plan might be: 'I'll make some music for these three chime bars. It'll be quiet at the beginning and then louder and quieter again'. (See also Flash (1990) for this way of working.)

These strategies parallel two opposite ways in which any composer might work: either deciding on an outline shape for the piece and then 'filling it in', or taking a musical motif or idea and developing it into a larger structure.

Recording and listening back is a useful way to follow up this work. Teacher and child can then talk about the music, describing what they hear. This helps children to build their musical understanding. Children themselves can choose to save music on tape from time to time and this also gives the teacher examples for assessment. Once a facility for recording has been established, it can become just a routine way of keeping track of pupils' learning.

listen for

- how timbre has been used;
- rhythmic and melodic ideas and patterns;
- musical structures: repeated ideas, ideas which are changed or varied, different sections in the music; children's sense of the piece as a whole;
- use of dynamics.

notice

- how much control of the instrument there is; development of technical skills;
- where the child's attention is; is it listening attention?
- whether music can be remembered and repeated;
- imaginative ideas in how the music is made.

It is a good idea to link children's music-making to listening to the music-making of others. Experiencing a wide range of music gives a richer store of musical ideas from which children's own imaginations can draw. The following is an example of a listening choice focusing on music made on one instrument. It is given in detail to demonstrate an approach which could be used with music of the teacher's own choice.

●————————————————————————————

mbira music from Zimbabwe played by Stella Rambisai Chiweshe with vocals, shaker, drumming
[Piranha-EFA CD 01892 26]

The mbira is a classic traditional instrument, found in many parts of Africa. Zimbabwe has one of the richest mbira traditions, a thousand year history of handed-down music.

This is music which can be mesmerising to listen to. The metal tongues of the instrument are plucked with great dexterity. The music is based on a continuous interplay of patterns which the ear can hardly keep up with. But the timbres which result are gentle, liquid and compelling. This is free-flowing music which shows us how music can take the listener over.

Mbira music will introduce children to a sound which is all of its own and which many will never have heard before (Marx, 1990). It would be a good choice as part of work on different timbres or on how an instrument itself suggests the music that can be played on it.

This recording is chosen because Stella Rambisai Chiweshe is known in Zimbabwe as 'The Queen of Mbira'. She is unusual in that she combines traditional music making with hi-tech recording of pop arrangements. The cultural roots of this music are in ceremony and ritual. As a traditional Maridzambira (Mbira Musician), Stella Rambisai Chiweshe has played at ceremonies three nights each weekend for more than 20 years. This CD combines mbira with other instruments, with Rambisai's own vocals. It includes call and response music [e.g. track 3: Gova Rine Mhanda] which makes a good introduction to another song structure which is found across many cultures.

<table>
<tr><td>

starting points

</td><td>

An ideal starting point would be to find a quietening down time, close eyes and just listen, letting the children become absorbed just in the sound.

[E.g. track 7: Chakwi. In this example there's an opening section with just mbira; then other instruments join in. This is an idea for how to start a piece gradually. Finally Rambisai sings over the top, a song in which every phrase has a falling pattern. The tune of the song is in the mbira part too but bound up with all the patternings. Eventually ululation is added over the top, an almost supernatural kind of voice sound.]

Find adjectives to describe what you heard. '*How would you tell someone who hadn't heard it what this instrument sounded like?*' Another introduction would be to look closely at an mbira or related instrument, or even a picture of one, and talk about how it could be played and what it might sound like. Imagine the sounds in your head. Then listen.

</td></tr>
</table>

investigate

- the idea of music based on a continuous flow of sound, or on repeated patternings; *What is it like to listen to this? What effect does it have on you?*
- how the voice is used; *what kinds of vocal sound do you hear?*
- the way the song is shaped; *what kind of pitch shapes (up and down) do you hear? do the words repeat?*
- the idea of a handed-on tradition of music; *how would you learn the music? who from?*
- the idea of being a virtuoso performer; *how long would it take to learn to play like this?*

go on to

Look for musical connections between how this music is made, partly traditional, partly improvised, and the music children have made.

For young children, if improvisation and composing is to progress, plenty of opportunity is needed for working alone, individually. Even when one child cooperates with another, with both enjoying the feeling of making music together, the actual music made is often essentially solo music. Each child pursues their own ideas, albeit alongside each other. Musical, as opposed to social, cooperation comes later. If all music making is done in groups, this slows down the learning process considerably.

Classroom organisation, therefore, needs to allow for individuals to have turns working with instruments, and to have turns with different instruments on different occasions. Children playing alone do not, on the whole, make very much noise; more importantly still from the musical point of view, they can hear the music they're making.

sorting sound

Identifying sorts of instruments and encouraging children to find their own ways of sorting and categorising them can be a rich source of learning in both composition and performing. Hornböstel and Sachs (1940) established categories for classifying world instruments which are more useful as a starting point than the familiar orchestral ones, although they have names which are not particularly amenable:

- aerophones: *wind instruments, where sound is produced by the vibration of air; e.g. pipes, flutes, reeds, whistles, ocarinas, brass, mouth organs;*

- chordophones: *stringed instruments, where sound is produced by the vibration of strings; e.g. fiddle, harp, zither, guitar, viols and violins, bows, and strung keyboards;*

- idiophones: *made of material that is naturally sonorous without being stretched or altered; e.g. rattles, jingles, claves, bells, gongs, xylophones, metallophones, scrapers, mbira;*

- membranophones: *where the sound is produced by the vibration of a stretched skin; e.g. drums of every kind, kazoos;*

- electrophones: *where the sound is produced by means of an electrical current; e.g. guitars, keyboards, synthesisers, electric fiddles, computers.*

Not only do these allow us to group instruments from any musical culture or style on a common basis, they also help to focus on the basic technologies involved in the making of all instruments. Deriving from the basis of how the sound is produced, they are a useful starting point for exploring the science of sound and the skills of making and controlling it. These categories can be used to make sure that some instruments of each type are included in the classroom collection, and that instrumental work and music listened to covers the full range. With older children, the categories themselves can be used for investigating instruments and their sounds and technologies, taking a cross-cultural perspective.

Sorting instruments is a way of helping children begin to organise their experience of the sound of sound, the timbre which different instrumental groupings offer. It goes hand in hand with the ongoing process of investigating the potential of individual instruments as it becomes clearer to children how the sound is made and what musical characteristics will follow. Sorting activities help to focus children's listening and clarify the range of techniques which can be used to make sounds with particular instruments.

For young children beginning to explore instruments the following ways of sorting work well:
- according to how the instrument is played: *blown, struck, shaken, plucked, scraped;*
- according to the material the instrument is made of: *wood, metal, skin;*
- according to size: *larger or smaller of same or different 'families';*
- according to shape.

Often instruments will fall into more than one category and this leads to further discoveries. Children can be encouraged to invent their own ways of sorting; these nearly always reveal something relevant to musical purposes, however unlikely they seem.

Sorting activities must be followed through into musical activity if children are to be helped to increase their sensitivity to instrumental sound as composers, listeners and performers. Each of the categories above leads to a characteristic kind of musical sound palette and these can be used as starting points for improvising and composing:
- music for rattles and shakers: *this gives infinitely varied*

resonances depending on shape and density of container/ resonator and on weight and shape of seeds or beads inside or outside; dynamic range, texture and rhythm might be the main musical characteristics;

● music for wood or for metal: *wood sounds are characteristically short, while metal sounds have a longer decay time; the rhythmic element of music with these two groups might be rather different; music in either group could combine pitched or unpitched instruments;*

● music for skin on skin (hand drumming): *this music could draw on a very wide range of hand and finger sounds and the different pitches available from different sized drums and different parts of the drum head;*

● music for small instruments: *might be characterised by a higher pitched sound spectrum.*

Sorting instruments leads easily into sorting sounds, and close connections will arise as can be seen above. Sorting and investigating sound itself is often better approached on a comparative basis: 'longer than and shorter than' rather than 'long and short'. This can be a useful focus for getting to know any individual instrument better as it concentrates attention on how sound from an instrument can be controlled and the different playing techniques available.

Exploration of instruments and making music with them can be supported by listening to the widest possible range of music for different instruments and for 'sorted sound'. Here is a detailed example; a similar approach could be applied to other music in the school collection.

● ───

Super Percussion of India
[CD World Music Library. King record co Ltd. KICC 5113]

The Indian tabla is a pair of tunable drums, one larger, one smaller. Like other instruments used within the North Indian classical music tradition, tabla take a life-time to learn. Tabla music offers a good way to introduce children to the possibilities of hand-drumming, to the scope offered by two drums played side by side but of different sizes, and to the timbre and pitch patterns that arise from hitting the drum in different places and with different parts of the hand and fingers.

This recording is chosen because it includes a tabla solo by Zakir Hussain, one of India's greatest tabla players, and also an example of Southern Indian rhythmic music for ghatam (a jar-like instrument) played by T.H. Vinayakram and kanjira (tambourine), played by Govindarao Harishankar. Whilst the playing skills are extraordinary, these are instruments to which children can relate directly. Best of all would be to see musicians playing this music live and to gain an idea of how an improvisation develops within a given framework. In group music this entails a great deal of interaction between players.

| starting points |

One starting point is to listen and discover that there are vocal syllables through which the different drum sounds can be indicated. Rhythm patterns can be memorised with the help of these sound syllables. Children can learn just a couple and work out some patternings of their own which they can say rhythmically.
[Track 1: This tabla solo starts with some vocal patterning. It is fast and energetic, using all kind of patternings of different hand and finger attacks.]

Another way in is to collect as many examples as you can find of 'double' instruments: bongo drums, two-tone bells or wooden agogo. Investigate these to discover how the two parts are different – smaller – higher? Make some two-pitch patterns of your own.

Alternatively, find out how many different finger and hand sounds you can find, using just one fairly large drum. Practise making patterns out of two or more ways of striking the drum head. Then listen to the music.

[A second track on this CD is a duet between the ghatam and kanjira. The two timbres are contrasted so it is easy to hear the two parts. The metre is counted 12 123; this gives a chance to get the feel of a less familiar patterning.]

| investigate |

• the idea of so many different sounds from each instrument that they're almost like voices;

- the idea of making up rhythm patterns as you go along;
- the idea of changing rhythm and timbre patterns as you go along;
- ways two players might make up music together;
- the skill these players have: how do they learn? how do they practise? what is difficult about playing tabla, kanjira, ghatam?
- the sound of skin, pot, metal jingles;
- how a concert performance of this music might develop.

accompanying singing with instruments

Once children have had some initial experience in the use of a range of instruments, these can be incorporated into class music-making as accompaniment for singing. Playing instruments in large groups is harder to do and harder to manage than voice work in the early stages. To combine one or two instruments with singing a song can work well if it is introduced in a simple way and time given for plenty of practice. Songs with accompaniments can be kept 'in repertoire' and revisited frequently enough for players to become confident and skilled. A very common mistake with music is to stop playing or singing it as soon as children 'get it right'. In fact, most of the learning value comes once children know the music well enough to listen and experience the music fully.

The following aspects should be taken into account:
- Decide what role the accompanying instrument(s) might have;
  Roughly in order of difficulty this might be:
  playing along in any way you like;
  keeping a steady beat (not the word rhythm of the song);
  holding a drone (all on one note);
  repeating a rhythm pattern all the way through(use a word pattern);
  repeating a melodic pattern all the way through(as in a round);
  adding particular sound effects 'on cue';
  playing parts or all of the melody.

- Choose the instrument(s) to match the song;
  Choose an instrument for its timbre, and for the role it's going to play. Involve children in discussing these choices, e.g. What kind of sound would go well with this song? Which instrument would be good for keeping a beat?

- Decide when the instrument(s) might play.
  This might be:
  > *playing in the chorus and not in the verse (or vice versa);*
  > *playing at the beginning of each line, or at certain strategic points;*
  > *several instruments playing at different times;*
  > *playing an introduction, a bit in the middle, or an ending.*

These are all decisions about interpretation and performance. Involve children in making these choices. Try ideas out, listen and decide. It is a matter of imagination and judgment, not right and wrong.

| listen for | children's ability to: |

- control the instrument well enough to play their part;
- keep their music going;
- keep their music going in time with the singing;
- respond to stops, starts, changes in dynamics and speed.

playing in a group

As children gain more control over the instruments that are available, they will be ready to take part in group playing organised by the teacher.

There are two musical reasons for groupwork:
- to allow for music made with different combinations of sounds and instruments;
- to allow for music which has more than one part at a time and interaction between players.

When young children play together with instruments informally, just occasionally comes a wonderful moment when suddenly and quite intuitively they find a common beat and all are as one. The surprise and delight with which they react to this as recognition dawns is telling. To be musically together in this sense is a new and exciting experience. In the early stages it cannot easily be repeated to order.

Teachers can introduce groupwork with instruments while children are still at this stage as a way of introducing the skills of working musically together. This works well as long as it is accepted that 'together', for young children, may not sound like 'together' for adults.

Playing groups are best kept small, six to eight children at most. If the teacher needs the whole class together, it is best to have a large group of listeners sitting in a circle with a small group of players in the middle. Rotate children's turn to play and turns with different instruments. Smaller groups enable children to hear better what they're playing, but if all children need to be active, voice sounds, hand clapping etc. can be used as instrumental sound too.

activities

To begin with, children can play to a fairly free plan. For example:

- starting and stopping on a given signal, listening to the sound and the silence;
- getting gradually louder and quieter on a given signal, listening to keep the music smooth;
- each child plays for a short turn, one at a time round the circle;
- children in two 'sorted sound' groups e.g. shakers and plucked sounds, play on a signal, alternately;
- children try to keep a beat together.

These plans can be devised by the children, with new and interesting 'rules' added as children think about how they would like the music to sound. The learning aim at this stage is to get used to playing with others and synchronising playing actions to some degree.

notice

differences between children's abilities to:

- control their instrument as the music requires;
- listen and play at the same time;
- listen to the group sound and adapt their own.

joining in

With some experience behind them children will be ready to try a 'joining-in' piece. To begin with, it may be easier for the teacher to join in and be the first to play.

    One player begins. The others listen and then join in one at a time. Don't rush to join in too soon. Listen to the music that's already going on before deciding what to play. Continue playing and try to keep listening. Discuss and try out different ways of finishing the music, for example:
dropping out in turn;
watching the first player and stopping all together when they do;
fading out the music gradually.

To begin with, an adult listening will need to suspend ideas of what 'fits'. At first, let children get used to the structure and their part in it. It's useful to have a listener or a listening group to talk about what they heard when the music stops. Very young or inexperienced children may not be able to make their part fit with other people's at all. This may be because they can't predict what their music will sound like, or because they have trouble coordinating their actions. They may not be able to take on board what other people are doing. See this as a beginning stage.

In any case, some aspects of music are easier to fit in with than others and it is a long process of development to reach the stage of being able to improvise coherently with other players. In the early stages, focus on timbres and the dynamics of the music as a whole; then consider the balance of one instrument against another. Are some instruments much louder than others? Children might decide to have one instrument in the background and others more to the fore. As children gain experience, roughly speaking, rhythmic fit comes sooner than melodic or harmonic fit.

    plan and try 'rules' for how the music can develop: e.g. each player plays a pattern which repeats all the way through; players can stop playing and start again later; players will listen to one instrument and follow its changes of speed and loudness (as in gamelan music);

- plan joining in music for a particular category of instruments (see above: sorting sound); listen and think about the different musical ideas which work for these instruments e.g. rattles and shakers could be used with a rhythmic beat or more freely to gradually build up a colour wash of sound;

- plan the order in which instruments join in according to how they sound and what they're playing;

- think about giving each instrument a different role e.g. one to keep a steady beat and one to play a rhythm pattern over it; one to play higher, shorter sounds and one to play lower, slower sounds;

- use tuned instruments with a chosen set of notes to begin to explore different scales and modes; e.g. [DEFA] [DEFGA] [DEGAB] [EFGBC] [CDEFG].

Record the music and listen to it. Talk about how it sounds.
Vocabulary: *adding a part, playing together, fitting in, layers, texture.*

listen for	

- indications that children are listening to themselves and to each other;
- what each child chooses to play: think about each musical element;
- indications of children finding ways to fit in with what's being played;
- control of the sounds produced; indications that the music is as the children intend.

This introduces an interactive musical structure, based on the idea of adding sounds in layers. Children get used to the sound and feel of playing at the same time as someone else and can gradually learn to listen to the music as a whole and not just their own part. Joining in introduces the musical element of texture. The different textures created by choice of instrument, by instruments of different pitch range and by what each instrument is doing can be explored. The overall structure of adding and subtracting parts to the music as it goes along is used by many composers and in many forms of group based music.

Listen to examples of joining-in music e.g. Ravel's Bolero is probably the best known classical piece based on the principle of joining in.

music for two

With plenty of initial experiences of working in a small group, children will be ready to extend their independent composing or performing activity to music for two players.

Working with two players playing together opens up the opportunity to devise a new set of musical structures and possibilities. Each of the examples below introduces both a musical structure and the performing role that goes with it. Children acquire performing skills which are specific to their role within the structure and are introduced to some different ways in which music can be constructed.

Be flexible about the management of this kind of work. Ideas for two players can be introduced with the class as a whole in a circle time or with a smaller group, demonstrated with one or two pairs only, and then followed up later, two at a time. Each child need not have a turn at each activity. Older children can work on their own; younger children will need a helper/listener. Older children could make a very simple piece of their own and teach it to a younger pair.

activities

keeping together

~ Try playing the same thing at the same time e.g. just a beat; a rhythm pattern; a melody idea; this helps to focus on the skills of keeping with someone else.

taking turns

~ Choose two instruments which make an interesting combination. A drum, xylophone or similar could be shared if each child has a beater.
Start by practising taking turns, with children making the music up as they go along.

Concentrate on learning how to take turns and on starting and stopping each turn so that the music keeps going. Turns can be shorter or longer, but not too long! Turns can be the same length (roughly) or different lengths. Listen to how the music sounds in each case.

progression

Go on to try different ways of taking turns e.g.

• take turns, copying: B roughly copies what A does, using the same rhythm or melodic shape, or dynamic character;

- take turns, having a conversation: A and B vary turns 'talking' in music; focus on playing differently but listening to each other and replying;
- take turns, going on from: B listens to A and continues it; again the focus might be on one or more musical elements.

Record the music and listen to it. Talk about how it sounds.

Vocabulary: *your turn, my turn; copy; same, similar, different, opposite; echo; answer.*

Listen to other examples:
   Monteverdi e.g. Deposuit in the Magnificat from the 1610 Vespers.
   Purcell e.g. Echo Dance in The Fairy Queen.

listen for

- indications that children are listening to themselves and to each other;
- the ways in which melody, rhythm, dynamics and tempo are used;
- children connecting to each others' musical ideas;
- control of the sounds produced; indications that the music is as the children intend.

children's learning

This introduces the idea of interacting with another player, by listening and adapting responses musically. This is a key skill in any music making with other people. It also introduces turn-taking as a basic musical structure. Even in music where there are more than two players, melodic or rhythmic ideas are often passed between different instruments and either copied or changed. Two instruments may build up music between them, sharing a melody or contrasting dynamic shapes. Or music may be based on echoes. Call and response songs also use a turn-taking structure.

activity

melody over a drone

- Find two pitched instruments. One could be a single chime bar.

   Child A holds a single note, say D, beating it as a steady(ish) beat on a xylophone, holding it down on a keyboard, keeping it ringing on a big chime bar, blowing it on an ocarina or recorder, taking breath when needed. This gives the drone as a harmonic basis to the music.

On the second instrument, child B makes a melody pattern or melodic line which moves over the top of the drone or around the drone note, so that the drone becomes the accompaniment to the tune. The melody might start on the drone note or return to it or might move away from and back to it as the music goes on. A note set can be chosen for the melody to use; with the drone on D this could be DFGA or DEFG or CDE, always with D as the centre.

Try to listen to each other and hear the effect of the two parts together. Record the music and listen to it. Talk about how it sounds.

progression

- make a rhythm pattern on the drone note or pattern it by stressing the first of every 3, 4 or 5 notes;
- play some or all of a known song tune over the drone – almost any simple melody will work if you can find a drone note or the key note which matches it. (This is particularly appropriate for beginner recorder or piano players who've already learnt one or two tunes).

Record the music and listen to it. Talk about how it sounds.
Vocabulary: *drone, melody, staying still on one pitch, moving up and down, by step or by jump, accompaniment.*

listen for

- each part separately and both together;
- rhythmic coordination; (this music can work without it if the children aren't ready; the essence of a drone is a kind of timeless foundation to the music);
- the steadiness of the drone;
- how B shapes the melody, the sound of the melody moving against the drone, sometimes dissonant against it sometimes not.

children's learning
- idea of two different melodic parts; a drone as the most basic beginning of harmony; idea of an accompaniment to a melody;
- link to traditional folk musics; instruments incorporating drones e.g. bagpipes, hurdy-gurdy; medieval dance music; Indian classical tradition.

learning instrumental skills

Finding sounds initially in an exploratory way is exciting and stimulating to the musical imagination. We respond to timbre as we do to colour and can enjoy it in a very similar way. Being able to produce and control sounds which are interesting and aesthetically pleasing involves acquiring skills in the use of instruments. Teachers need to help and encourage children in this long process and this can be done in a number of ways.

The beginnings of skill acquisition are founded in exploratory play and familiarisation with the shape and sound possibilities each particular instrument offers. Best of all is if this also includes seeing and hearing the instrument played by someone else, however simply; this allows time to take in both sounds and actions experienced as cause and effect. Controlling sound rests on an understanding of which actions cause which sounds and then the ability to control the action skilfully enough to produce the kind of sound desired at the right moment. Ultimately it involves being able to sustain this throughout a piece, modifying every sound in subtle detail to carry the interpretative and expressive intention.

Help children to focus on the playing actions required by each instrument. Each kind of instrument requires its own particular set of playing actions; instruments of the same kind but different sizes demand different degrees of finger dexterity, physical strength etc. Some commonly required actions are:

- striking, tapping, a smaller or larger surface with hand: *aiming for a particular part of the surface, controlling degree of force, controlling speed of attack and of taking beater off the surface;*
- striking individual notes or a larger surface with a hand held beater: *aiming strike, controlling force of it, travelling between one note and another; using two sticks at a time;*
- shaking: *controlling speed and force of movement; preventing unpredictable sounds;*
- scraping: *controlling speed, force and length of the movement;*
- blowing: *controlling the direction, shape and force of a stream of air;*
- plucking: *selecting the string or metal tongue on an mbira, controlling the force of movement, using different parts of fingertip or a plectrum;*

- pressing notes on a keyboard: *using fingers individually, moving between notes, controlling speed of attack, (depending on keyboard) controlling length and degree of pressure.*

A further set of actions is needed to modify or stop the sound e.g.
- changing pitch of notes by covering and uncovering holes on a recorder or ocarina;
- stopping notes on a string or sliding along it;
- 'damping' the sound e.g. with fingers or flat hand to end it before it has died naturally.

With any instrument, a part of learning to produce the sound can come fairly naturally with experience e.g. how hard to strike, but much is a matter of learning techniques which work well and this needs time and some guidance. To help children build instrumental skills, teachers can:
- encourage children to listen and modify their actions, noticing how these affect the sound;
- make opportunities for practising two or three actions on a chosen instrument;
- discuss what 'getting better' is like; notice and talk about what works well for a particular effect;
- show children standard central techniques (e.g. Cotton, 1996);
- play classroom instruments for children to listen to and watch;
- use video or live performers to watch and look for playing techniques.

Go as far as time allows in treating this aspect of instrumental playing seriously from the beginning. Allow children to stay with a single instrument over time and use it enough to become confident and adept at handling it. Children, like the rest of us, have often quite strong individual preferences for particular instruments – as listeners and as players. Allow them to find and follow these whilst keeping some breadth of experience in the early stages. Above all, encourage skill development towards musical ends and not as a separate part of learning.

Young children have endless patience with skill acquisition in play contexts or where the motivation is there. They are used to having to try endless times before succeeding fully and if this can be capitalised on it helps a lot. You have to be allowed to do most things badly in order to be able to do them well.

assessment points

early stages

The child:

- responds to instrumental timbre and dynamics and uses these musically;
- can make and perform music using patternings with a variety of instruments;
- can listen with awareness and sort and control sounds made by tuned and untuned instruments.

later stages

The child:

- understands the qualities of instrumental sound in relation to the elements of music;
- can improvise, compose and perform instrumental music, alone and with others;
- shows skills in controlling instrumental sound within a range of musical contexts.

early stages

The child:
- can find a singing voice and join in with singing the melody of known songs;
- can improvise songs or spontaneous singing conversations with a partner;
- can begin to control the voice in simple voice techniques (some control of breathing, producing a range of different voice sounds, standing well);
- can sing a number of one-liner and other short songs independently;
- responds to instrumental timbre and dynamics and uses these musically;
- can make and perform music using patternings with a variety of instruments;
- can listen with awareness and sort and control sounds made by tuned and untuned instruments;
- responds to music with movement and can match movements to the overall mood, dynamic and tempo of the piece;
- can improvise movements for music work with freedom and imagination, using some variety of movement vocabulary;
- has some skills for music movement work; can stop and start with control, and move in space with awareness for others;
- can give attention to and follow the music;
- can respond to music with interest and in a variety of ways;
- can pick out some aspects of the music and talk about them;
- can make and understand connections between simple notations and musical sounds.

later stages

The child:
- can sing short songs with accuracy and in tune with a given pitch;
- can make-up improvised and composed songs;
- can control the voice in first voice techniques (how to breath, stand well, singing tone);
- knows and can sing independently a range of songs, some from different places and times;

- understands the qualities of instrumental sound in relation to the elements of music;
- can improvise, compose and perform instrumental music, alone and with others;
- shows skills in controlling instrumental sound within a range of musical contexts;
- responds to music in movement and can match movements to the musical elements of beat, tempo and dynamics;
- can improvise movements to lead a music composition which show awareness in movement of contrasts in dynamics, a sense of timing and phrasing;
- has a varied movement vocabulary for music/movement work which is used with control and coordination;
- can follow music, listening for particular features;
- can ask questions, notice features and talk about these and their own responses;
- is building knowledge of the contexts in which music is made and can relate music's characteristics to this;
- can make and understand connections between notations and musical sounds in relation to each musical element.

books and resources

Barrs, K. (1994) *Music Works: Music in the Classroom 5-9*. Twickenham: Belair.

Baxter, K. and Thompson, K. (1988) *Pompaleerie Jig*. Leeds: E.J. Arnold.
A collection of music games.

Binns, T. (1994) *Children Making Music*. Hemel Hempstead: Simon and Schuster Education.

Bright Ideas (1987) *Language Resources*. Bright Ideas Teacher Handbooks. Leamington Spa: Scholastic.
Songs, games, counting rhymes for music and language.

Bright Ideas for Early Years (1991) *Music and Movement*. Leamington Spa: Scholastic.

Cotton, M. (1996) *Agogo Bells to Xylophone: A Friendly Guide to Classroom Percussion Instruments*. London: A & C Black.

Davies, L. (1993) *Take Note! A Music Handbook for Primary Teachers*. London: BBC Educational Publishing.

Durrant, C. and Welch, G. (1995) *Making Sense of Music*. London: Cassell.

East, H. (1989) *The Singing Sack*. London: A & C Black.
28 song-stories from around the world.

East, H. (1990) *Look Lively, Rest Easy*. London: A & C Black.
Songs, stories, tricks and rhymes to rouse and to relax.

Gilbert, J.(1981) *Musical Starting Points with Young Children*. London: Ward Lock.

Glover, J. and Ward, S. eds. (1993) *Teaching Music in the Primary School*. London: Cassell. Second edition (1998).

Holdstock, J. (1986 on) *Earwiggos*. Tadcaster: Holdstock/Lovely Music.
6 booklets of starter activities.

Holdstock, J. & Richards, C. (1995) *Sounds Topical*. Oxford: Oxford University Press.

Meek, B. (1989) *Moonpenny*. Cork: Ossian Publications.
A collection of rhymes, songs and play-verse for and by children gathered in Ireland.

Mills, J. (1991) *Music in the Primary School*. Cambridge: Cambridge University Press.

Odam, G. (1994) *Sound and Symbol*. Cheltenham: Stanley Thornes.

Richards, C. (1995) *Listen to This! Key Stage 1*. Saydisc Records, Chipping Manor, The Chipping, Wotton-Under-Edge, Glos. GL12 7AD.
Compact disc or cassette of musical examples accompanied by book.

Shepherd, M. (1989) *Music is Childsplay*. Harlow: Longman

Shreeves, R. (1991) *Children Dancing*. London: Ward Lock Educational.

Taylor, D. (1995) *Targeting Music*. London: Schott.
A year-by-year series for teachers in primary schools.

Tillman, J. (1983) *Kokoleoko, Songs and Activities for Children*. London and Basingstoke: MacMillan Education.

Primary Music Today Magazine: Peacock Press, Scout Bottom Farm, Mytholmroyd, Hebden Bridge. HX7 5JS.

References

Section 1

Drummond, M.J. (1993) *Assessing Children's Learning.* London: Fulton.

Kelly, L. and Sutton-Smith, B.(1987) 'A study of infant musical productivity', in J.C. Peery and I.W. Peery (eds) *Music in Child Development.* New York: Springer-Verlag.

Nicholson, M. (1995) *Composing in the Early Years.* Unpublished individual study. Roehampton Institute London.

Paley, V.G. (1990) *The Boy Who Would Be a Helicopter.* Cambridge, Massachusetts: Harvard University Press.

Papousek, M. (1996) 'Intuitive parenting: a hidden source of musical stimulation in infancy', in I. Deliege and J. Sloboda (eds) *Musical Beginnings.* Oxford: Oxford University Press.

Robson, S. (1996) 'Home and school: a potentially powerful partnership', in S. Robson and S. Smedley (eds) *Education in Early Childhood: First Things First.* London: Fulton.

Siraj-Blatchford, I. (1994) *The Early Years: Laying the Foundations for Racial Equality.* London: Trentham Books.

Hurst, B. et al. (1995) *Profiling, Recording and Observing: A Resource Pack for the Early Years.* London: Routledge.

Woodward, S. (1994) 'The window of opportunity'. Paper presented at the International Society for Music Education Early Childhood Commission Seminar, *Vital Connections: Young Children, Adults and Music.* Missouri, USA.

Woodward, S. et al. (1996) 'The birth of musical language'. Paper presented at the International Society for Music Education Early Childhood Commission Seminar, *Universal and Particular Elements of Early Childhood Music Education.* Winchester, UK.

Section 3

Wittgenstein, L. ed. Barrett, C. (1978) *Lectures & Conversations on Aesthetics, Psychology and Religious Belief.* Oxford: Blackwell.

Section 4

Davies, M. (1995) *Helping Children to Learn through a Movement Perspective.* London: Hodder and Stoughton.

Lloyd, H. (1964) sleeve notes: Topic Record

Metz, E. (1989) 'Movement as a musical response among preschool children', *Journal of Research in Music Education,* 37(1).

Opie, I. and Opie P. (1985) *The Singing Game.* Oxford: Oxford University Press.

Vanderspar, E. (undated) *Dalcroze Handbook: Principles and Guidelines for Teaching Eurhythmics.* mimeo.

Young, S. (1993) 'Physical movement: Its place in music education', *British Journal of Music Education,* 9(3) Cambridge: Cambridge University Press.

Young, S. (1996) 'Contributions to an understanding of the music and movement connection', *Early Child Development and Care,* **115**.

Section 6

Mahoney, D. (1997) 'Like a duck to water...listening and appraising', *Primary Music Today,* **7.** Hebden Bridge: Peacock Press.

Moog, H. (1976) *The Musical Experience of the Pre-school Child.* London: Schott.

Scruton, R. (1983) 'Representation in Music', in *The Aesthetic Understanding.* London: University Paperback.

Section 7

Athey, C. (1990) *Extending Thought in Young Children.* London: Paul Chapman Publishing.

Bamberger, J. (1994) 'Coming to hear in a new way', in R. Aiello and J. Sloboda (eds) *Musical Perceptions.* Oxford: Oxford University Press.

Blenkin, G. and Kelly, V. (1996) 'Education as development', in G. Blenkin and A.V. Kelly (eds) *Early Childhood Education: A Developmental Curriculum.* Second Edition. London: Paul Chapman.

Donaldson, M. (1978) *Children's Minds.* London: Fontana.

Edwards, C., Gandini, L. and Forman, G. (1995) *The Hundred Languages of Children: The Reggio Emilia Approach to Early Childhood Education.* New Jersey: Ablex.

Flash, L. (1990) 'Changing perceptions of music with reception children', *British Journal of Music Education,* 7(1) Cambridge: Cambridge University Press.

Forrai, K. (1974) translated and adapted by J. Sinor (1988) *Music in Preschool.* Budapest: Corvina.

Glynne-Jones, M. (1974) *Schooling in the Middle Years: Music*, London: MacMillan.

Gura, P. (ed.) (1992) *Exploring Learning: Young Children and Blockplay*. London: Paul Chapman.

Gura, P. (1996) *Resources for Early Learning: Children, Adults and Stuff*. London: Hodder and Stoughton.

Hanke, M. (1994) *Face the Music: Key Concepts Simplified for the Class Teacher*. Hemel Hempstead: Simon and Schuster.

Stocks, M. and Maddocks, A. (1992) *Growing with Music. Key Stage 1: Teacher's Book*. Essex: Longman.

Young, S. (1992) 'Physical movement: Its place in music education', *British Journal of Music Education*. 9(3) Cambridge: Cambridge University Press.

Section 8

Adzenyah, A. et al. (1997) *Let your voice be heard! Songs from Ghana and Zimbabwe*. Danbury, CT: World Music Press.

Andress, B. (1980) *Music Experiences in Early Childhood*. New York: Holt, Rinehart and Winston.

Christian, P. and Burnett, M. (1981) 'Caribbean resource material', *Music Teacher*. June, 10-11.

Davies, C. (1986) 'Say it till a song comes', *British Journal of Music Education* 10(3). Cambridge: Cambridge University Press.

Davies, C. (1992) 'Listen to my song: A study of songs invented by children aged 5-7 years', *British Journal of Music Education* 8(1). Cambridge: Cambridge University Press.

Durrant, C. and Welch, G. (1995) *Making Sense of Music: Foundations for Music Education*. London: Cassell.

Glover, J. (1993) 'Assessing children's learning in music', in J. Glover and S. Ward (eds) *Teaching Music in the Primary School*. London: Cassell.

Hargreaves, D.J. (1986) *The Developmental Psychology of Music*. Cambridge: Cambridge University Press.

Moore, R. (1994) 'Selected research on children's singing skills', in G.F. Welch and T. Murao (eds) *Onchi and Singing Development: A Cross-cultural Perspective*. London: Fulton.

Opie, I. and Opie, P. (1985) *The Singing Game*. Oxford: Oxford University Press.

Suthers, L. (1996) 'Using puppetry to help toddlers find their singing voices. Paper presented at the International Society for Music Education Early Childhood Commission Seminar, *Universal and Particular Elements of Early Childhood Music Education*. Winchester, UK.

Tarnowski, S. (1994) 'Musical play of preschoolers and the effects of teacher–child interaction style on those behaviours'. Paper presented at the International Society for Music Education Early Childhood Commission Seminar, *Vital Connections: Young Children, Adults and Music*. Missouri, USA.

Victor-Smith, G. (1996) 'Singing in the early years', *Primary Music Today*, 4, 29-33, Hebden-Bridge: Peacock Press.

Welch, G.F. (1986) 'A developmental view of children's singing', *British Journal of Music Education*, 3(3). Cambridge: Cambridge University Press.

Welch, G. and Murao, T. (eds) (1994) *Onchi and Singing Development: A Cross-cultural Perspective*. London: Fulton.

Welch, G. F. (1997) 'The developing voice', in L. Thurman and G.F. Welch (eds) *Bodymind and Voice: Foundations of Voice Education*. Iowa: National Center for Voice and Speech.

Whitehead, M. (1996) *The Development of Language and Literacy*. London: Hodder and Stoughton.

Wright, J. (1996) 'Rhyme and reading', *Primary Music Today*, 6, 13-14. Hebden Bridge: Peacock Press.

Section 9

Cotton, M. (1996) *Agogo Bells to Xylophone: A Friendly Guide to Classroom Percussion Instruments*. London: A&C Black.

Dale, T. (1995) 'Musical play structures', *Primary Music Today* 1. Hebden Bridge: Peacock Press.

Ellis, P. (1987) 'Microelectronics in special education', *British Journal of Music Education* 4(1). Cambridge: Cambridge University Press.

Ellis, P. (1995) 'Sound therapy', *Primary Music Today* 3. Hebden Bridge: Peacock Press.

Flash, L. (1990) 'Changing perceptions of music with reception children', *British Journal of Music Education* 7(1). Cambridge: Cambridge University Press.

Glover, J. (1993) 'Assessing children's learning in music', in J. Glover and S. Ward (eds) *Teaching Music in the Primary School*. London: Cassell.

Marx, M. (1990) 'A Zimbabwean mbira: A tradition in African music and its potential for music education', *British Journal of Music Education* 7(1) Cambridge: Cambridge University Press.

Sachs, C. (1940) *The History of Musical Instruments*. New York: Norton.

index

6471